Quick & Easy

Published in 2011 by Murdoch Books Pty Limited.

Murdoch Books Pty Ltd
Pier 8/9, 23 Hickson Road,
Millers Point NSW 2000
Phone: + 61 (0) 2 8220 2000
Fax: + 61 (0) 2 8220 2558
www.murdochbooks.com.au

Murdoch Books UK Limited
Erico House, 6th Floor
93–99 Upper Richmond Road
Putney, London SW15 2TG
Phone: +44 (0)20 8785 5995
Fax: +44 (0)20 8785 5985
www.murdochbooks.co.uk

Publisher: Lynn Lewis
Project Manager: Liz Malcolm
Designer: Kylie Mulquin
Editor: Justine Harding
Production: Alexandra Gonzalez

National Library of Australia Cataloguing-in-Publication:
Title: Quick & Easy.
ISBN: 978-1-74266-509-2 (pbk.)
Series: Easy eats.
Notes: Includes index.
Subjects: Quick and easy cooking.
641.555

Printed by Hang Tai Printing Company Limited, China.
PRINTED IN CHINA

IMPORTANT: Those who might be at risk from the effects of salmonella poisoning (the elderly, pregnant women, young children and
those suffering from immune deficiency diseases) should consult their doctor with any concerns about eating raw eggs.

CONVERSION GUIDE: You may find cooking times vary depending on the oven you are using.
For fan-forced ovens, as a general rule, set the oven temperature to 20°C (35°F) lower than indicated in the recipe.

Quick & Easy

more than 100 recipes for the busy cook

MURDOCH BOOKS

Contents

Snacks & light meals

Low on time and big on flavour,
this selection of recipes caters perfectly
to the demands of busy people.

SPANISH TORTILLA

preparation time 20 minutes
cooking time 30 minutes
makes 16 wedges

125 ml (4 fl oz/½ cup) olive oil
2 large all-purpose potatoes, peeled
    and cut into 5 mm (¼ inch) slices
2 large onions, sliced
3 eggs

• Heat the oil in a 20 cm (8 inch) diameter deep non-stick frying pan with a
lid. Place alternate layers of potato and onion in the pan, cover and cook for
8 minutes over low heat. Using tongs, turn the layers in sections (it doesn't
matter if they break up). Cover and cook for 8 minutes, without allowing the
potato to colour.

• Put a strainer over a bowl and drain the potato mixture, reserving about
1 tablespoon of the oil.

• Put the eggs and a little salt and pepper in a bowl and whisk to combine.
Add the potato mixture, pressing down with the back of a spoon to completely
cover with the egg.

• Heat the reserved oil in the same frying pan over high heat. Pour in the egg
mixture, pressing down to even it out. Reduce the heat to low, cover with a lid
and cook for 12 minutes, or until set. Gently shake the pan to ensure the tortilla
is not sticking. Leave for 5 minutes, then invert onto a plate. Cut into wedges.
Serve at room temperature.

WARM EGGPLANT AND FETA SALAD

preparation time 5 minutes
cooking time 5 minutes
serves 4

10–12 Lebanese eggplants (small
    aubergines), trimmed
2 tablespoons olive oil
2 large handfuls mint
140 g (5 oz/1 cup) crumbled firm feta
    cheese
24 semi-dried tomatoes

YOGHURT DRESSING
125 g (4½ oz/½ cup) Greek-style
    yoghurt
1 teaspoon ground cumin
2 small garlic cloves, crushed

• To make the yoghurt dressing, combine the yoghurt, cumin, garlic and
1 tablespoon water in a small bowl and stir to combine well. Season to taste
with sea salt and freshly ground black pepper. Set aside.

• Cut the eggplants in half lengthways. Heat the oil in a heavy-based frying
pan over medium heat and cook the eggplant, cut side down, for 2 minutes,
then turn and cook for another 2 minutes or until cooked through. Place on
a serving plate, scatter over the mint, feta and tomatoes, drizzle with the
yoghurt dressing and serve immediately.

Snacks & light meals

BAKED EGGPLANT WITH TOMATO AND MOZZARELLA

preparation time 20 minutes
cooking time 40 minutes
serves 6

6 large slender eggplants
   (aubergines), halved lengthways,
   leaving the stems attached
100 ml (3½ fl oz) olive oil
2 onions, finely chopped
2 garlic cloves, crushed
400 g (14 oz) tinned chopped
   tomatoes

1 tablespoon tomato paste
   (concentrated purée)
3 tablespoons chopped flat-leaf
   (Italian) parsley
1 tablespoon chopped oregano
125 g (4½ oz) mozzarella cheese,
   grated

● Preheat the oven to 180°C (350°F/Gas 4). Score the eggplant flesh by cutting a crisscross pattern with a sharp knife, being careful not to cut through the skin. Heat 2 tablespoons of the oil in a large frying pan, add three eggplants and cook for 2–3 minutes each side, or until the flesh is soft. Remove. Repeat with another 2 tablespoons of the oil and the remaining eggplants. Cool slightly and scoop out the flesh, leaving a 2 mm (1/16 inch) border. Finely chop the eggplant flesh and reserve the shells.

● In the same pan, heat the remaining oil and cook the onion over medium heat for 5 minutes. Add the garlic and cook for 30 seconds, then add the tomato, tomato paste, parsley, oregano and eggplant flesh, and cook, stirring occasionally, over low heat for 8–10 minutes, or until the sauce is thick and pulpy. Season well. Arrange the eggplant shells in a lightly greased baking dish and spoon in the tomato filling. Sprinkle with mozzarella and bake for 5–10 minutes, or until the cheese has melted.

STUFFED MUSHROOMS

preparation time 10 minutes
cooking time 25 minutes
serves 4

8 large cap mushrooms
80 ml (2½ fl oz/⅓ cup) olive oil
30 g (1 oz) prosciutto, finely chopped
1 garlic clove, crushed
2 tablespoons soft fresh breadcrumbs

30 g (1 oz) freshly grated parmesan
  cheese
2 tablespoons chopped flat-leaf
  (Italian) parsley

● Preheat the oven to 190°C (375°F/Gas 5). Lightly grease a baking dish.
Remove the mushroom stalks and finely chop them.

● Heat 1 tablespoon of the oil in a frying pan, add the prosciutto, garlic and
mushroom stalks and cook for 5 minutes. Mix in a bowl with the breadcrumbs,
parmesan and parsley.

● Brush the mushroom caps with 1 tablespoon of the olive oil and place them,
gill side up, in the baking dish. Divide the stuffing among the caps and bake for
20 minutes. Drizzle with the remaining oil and serve hot or warm.

Snacks & light meals

CHICKEN AND BLACK BEAN SOUP WITH AVOCADO SALSA

preparation time 20 minutes
cooking time 35 minutes
serves 4–6

2 tablespoons olive oil
8 boneless, skinless chicken thighs
    (about 500 g/1 lb 2 oz), trimmed
    and cut into 2 cm (¾ inch) chunks
1 onion, finely chopped
2 carrots, finely chopped
2 celery stalks, thinly sliced
1 red capsicum (pepper), cut into
    1 cm (½ inch) pieces
1½ teaspoons ground cumin
½ teaspoon chilli powder, or to taste
1 teaspoon ground coriander
410 g (14½ oz) tinned black beans,
    rinsed and drained
150 g (5½ oz/1 cup) frozen corn
    kernels
1 litre (35 fl oz/4 cups) chicken stock
400 g (14 oz) tinned chopped
    tomatoes
125 g (4½ oz/½ cup) sour cream
2 large soft tortillas, warmed

AVOCADO SALSA

1 avocado, cut into 1 cm (½ inch)
    chunks
1 small handful coriander (cilantro)
    leaves, chopped
1 teaspoon finely grated lime rind
2 tablespoons lime juice

● Heat the olive oil in a large heavy-based saucepan or casserole dish over medium heat. Add the chicken and cook, stirring often, for 5–6 minutes, or until golden all over. Remove to a plate and set aside.

● Add the onion, carrot, celery and capsicum to the pan. Sauté for 5 minutes, or until the onion starts to soften. Add the spices and cook for 1 minute, or until fragrant, stirring constantly. Return the chicken to the pan and add the black beans, corn, chicken stock and tomatoes. Bring to the boil, then reduce the heat to medium–low and simmer for 20 minutes, until the chicken is tender.

● For the avocado salsa, put the avocado, coriander, lime rind and lime juice in a small bowl and gently mix together.

● Cut the tortillas into strips. Ladle the soup into warm deep bowls. Spoon a dollop of sour cream onto each. Top with a generous spoonful of the avocado salsa and the tortilla strips and serve.

SPICED CHICKEN QUESADILLAS

preparation time 10 minutes plus 1 hour marinating
cooking time 15 minutes
serves 4

2½ tablespoons extra virgin olive oil
½ teaspoon dried oregano
½ teaspoon ground cumin
2 tablespoons lime juice
1 boneless, skinless chicken breast
4 soft flour tortillas
60 g (2¼ oz/½ cup) grated
   cheddar cheese
60 g (2¼ oz/¼ cup) grilled red
   capsicum (pepper), cut into thin
   strips (available from the
   supermarket deli counter)

2 tablespoons pickled sliced
   jalapeños, chopped (available
   from the supermarket)
2 tablespoons chopped coriander
   (cilantro) leaves
2 tablespoons tomato salsa
2 tablespoons sour cream

• Combine 2 tablespoons of the olive oil with the oregano, cumin and lime juice in a bowl and whisk to combine well. Slice the chicken into 5 mm (¼ inch) strips, then add to the mixture in the bowl and toss to coat. Cover the bowl and refrigerate for 1 hour or until needed. Drain the chicken. Place a non-stick frying pan over medium heat and cook the chicken, stirring, for 5 minutes or until just cooked through. Remove the chicken from the pan and set aside.

• Place a tortilla on a board and sprinkle with some of the cheese. Top with some chicken, capsicum, jalapeños and coriander. Place a tortilla over the top and press down lightly. Repeat with the remaining tortillas and filling.

● Place a clean frying pan over medium–low heat, add the remaining oil and swirl to coat the base of the pan. Place one quesadilla in the pan and cook for 3–5 minutes, then carefully turn it over and cook for another 3 minutes or until the cheese has melted and the quesadilla is golden brown. Repeat with the remaining quesadillas.

● To serve, allow the quesadillas to cool slightly, then cut into wedges, and serve with the salsa and sour cream.

Snacks & light meals

DEEP-DISH CHICKEN PIZZA

preparation time 30 minutes plus 1 hour proving
cooking time 30 minutes
serves 4

1½ teaspoons active dry yeast
½ teaspoon caster (superfine) sugar
335 g (11¾ oz/2¼ cups) plain
   (all-purpose) flour, approximately
1 teaspoon sea salt
2 tablespoons finely grated parmesan
   cheese
1 tablespoon olive oil

TOPPING
125 ml (4 fl oz/½ cup) tomato passata
   (puréed tomatoes)
a pinch of caster (superfine) sugar
265 g (9½ oz/1½ cups) shredded
   cooked chicken
1 small handful basil, plus extra,
   to garnish
85 g (3 oz/⅓ cup) drained marinated
   roasted capsicum (pepper) strips
   (available from supermarkets)
2 bacon slices, cut into thin strips
200 g (7 oz) bocconcini (fresh baby
   mozzarella cheese), torn into
   chunks
olive oil, for drizzling (optional)

- Combine the yeast, sugar and 250 ml (9 fl oz/1 cup) lukewarm water in a small bowl and leave in a warm place for 10 minutes, or until foamy.

- Put the flour and salt in a large bowl, then stir in the parmesan, yeast mixture and oil. Turn out onto a lightly floured surface and knead for 5 minutes, or until the dough is smooth and elastic; if the dough is sticky you may need to add a little extra flour, but don't add too much or the dough will be tough. Place the dough in an oiled bowl, then cover and leave in a warm place for 1 hour, until the dough has doubled in size.

- Meanwhile, preheat the oven to 220°C (425°F/Gas 7). Lightly oil a round 28 cm (11 ¼ inch) baking tin that is at least 2.5 cm (1 inch) deep.

- Turn the dough out onto a lightly floured surface and knead briefly until smooth. Roll the dough out until large enough to cover the base and side of the tin; the dough will be fairly thick. Press the sides of the dough into the tin to fit.

- Mix together the passata and sugar and spread over the dough. Top with the chicken, basil, capsicum, bacon and bocconcini, then bake for 25–30 minutes, or until the dough is golden brown.

- Sprinkle with extra basil, cut into wedges and serve immediately, drizzled with a little olive oil if desired.

CHICKEN FALAFEL WITH TABOULEH CONES

preparation time 20 minutes
cooking time 20 minutes
makes 24

45 g (1½ oz/¼ cup) burghul (bulgar)
4 pieces lavash or other unleavened
    bread (23 x 30 cm/9 x 12 inch)
2 spring onions (scallions), thinly
    sliced
1 large tomato, seeded and finely
    chopped
1 small Lebanese (short) cucumber,
    finely chopped
1 large handful flat-leaf (Italian)
    parsley, chopped
1 tablespoon lemon juice
1 tablespoon virgin olive oil
1 tablespoon olive oil
1 onion, finely chopped

1 garlic clove, crushed
2 teaspoons ground coriander
1 teaspoon cumin seeds
½ teaspoon ground cinnamon
250 g (9 oz) minced (ground) chicken
300 g (10½ oz) tinned chickpeas,
    rinsed, drained and mashed
1 handful mint, chopped
1 handful flat-leaf (Italian) parsley,
    extra, chopped
2 tablespoons plain (all-purpose) flour
vegetable oil, for deep-frying
60 g (2¼ oz/¼ cup) Greek-style
    yoghurt

• Soak the burghul in hot water for 20 minutes. Cut the bread widthways into thirds, then cut in half. Keep the bread covered with a damp cloth to prevent it drying out. Cut 24 pieces of baking paper the same size as the bread. Roll the paper up around the bottom half of the bread to form a cone and secure. Twist at the bottom. You will need 24 bread cones.

● Drain the burghul in a fine mesh sieve, pressing out as much water as possible. Transfer to a bowl and mix with the spring onion, tomato, cucumber, parsley, lemon juice and virgin olive oil, and season.

● Heat the olive oil in a frying pan, add the onion and garlic and cook, stirring over medium−low heat, for 5 minutes, or until the onion is soft. Add the spices and cook for another minute, or until the spices are aromatic.

● Put the onion mixture, minced chicken, chickpeas, mint and extra parsley in a bowl, season and mix until combined. Shape into 24 firm falafel patties. Toss the falafel in the flour and shake off the excess.

● Fill a deep-fryer or heavy-based saucepan one-third full of oil and heat to 180°C (350°F), or until a cube of bread dropped into the oil turns golden brown in 15 seconds. Cook the falafels in batches for 3−4 minutes each side, or until golden and heated through. Drain on crumpled paper towels.

● To assemble, put a falafel in each bread cone and top with some tabouleh, then ½ teaspoon yoghurt.

Note   *The tabouleh is best made on the day of serving. The falafel can be prepared up to a day ahead and cooked just before serving.*

CHINESE DUCK PANCAKES WITH FIVE-SPICE AND HOISIN

preparation time 20 minutes
cooking time 30 minutes
serves 4

150 g (5½ oz/1 cup) plain
    (all-purpose) flour
2 tablespoons cornflour (cornstarch)
1 tablespoon sesame seeds
125 ml (4 fl oz/½ cup) milk
2 eggs
2 teaspoons sesame oil

2 Chinese barbecued duck breasts
vegetable oil, for pan-frying
4 spring onions (scallions), cut into
    5 cm (2 inch) lengths
1 Lebanese (short) cucumber, seeded
    and cut into thin strips
125 ml (4 fl oz/½ cup) hoisin sauce

- In a bowl, mix together the flour, cornflour, sesame seeds and a pinch of sea salt, then make a well in the centre. Whisk together the milk, eggs, sesame oil and 125 ml (4 fl oz/½ cup) water, then gradually whisk into the flour mixture until smooth. Cover with plastic wrap and allow to rest for 20 minutes.

- Meanwhile, thinly slice the duck breasts and set aside.

- Heat a non-stick frying pan over medium heat. Lightly brush with vegetable oil. Spoon 2 tablespoons of the batter into the pan and spread to make a thin pancake, about 15 cm (6 inches) in diameter. Cook for 1 minute, then turn the pancake over and cook for a further 30 seconds. Remove to a plate and repeat with the remaining batter to make 20 pancakes, brushing the pan with some more oil as needed.

- Place 2 duck breast strips, 2 spring onion pieces and 2 cucumber strips on each pancake. Drizzle each with 1 teaspoon hoisin sauce and roll up. Serve immediately, with the remaining hoisin sauce.

BEEF NACHOS TOPPED WITH AVOCADO CREAM

preparation time 20 minutes
cooking time 35 minutes
serves 4

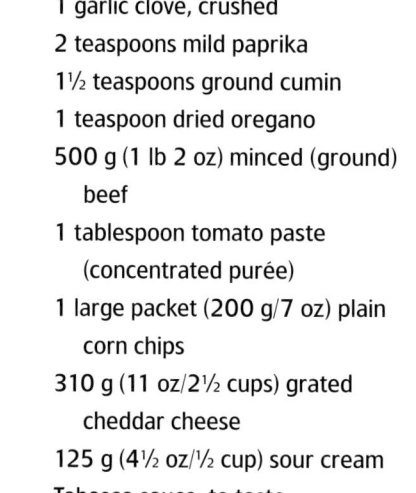

800 g (1 lb 12 oz) tinned chopped
    tomatoes
1 small handful coriander (cilantro)
    leaves
1 large mild green banana chilli or
    small green capsicum (pepper),
    seeds removed, flesh chopped
1 tablespoon peanut oil
4 spring onions (scallions), finely sliced
1 garlic clove, crushed
2 teaspoons mild paprika
1½ teaspoons ground cumin
1 teaspoon dried oregano
500 g (1 lb 2 oz) minced (ground)
    beef
1 tablespoon tomato paste
    (concentrated purée)
1 large packet (200 g/7 oz) plain
    corn chips
310 g (11 oz/2½ cups) grated
    cheddar cheese
125 g (4½ oz/½ cup) sour cream
Tabasco sauce, to taste
sliced jalapeño chillies, to serve

2 spring onions (scallions), finely sliced
coriander (cilantro) leaves, to serve

AVOCADO CREAM
1 large ripe avocado
1 tablespoon lemon juice
125 g (4½ oz/½ cup) sour cream

- Preheat the oven to 180°C (350°F/Gas 4).

- Put the tomatoes, coriander and green chilli or capsicum in a food processor and blend until smooth.

- Heat the peanut oil in a large frying pan over medium–high heat. Add the spring onion, garlic, spices and oregano and cook, stirring, for 1 minute. Add the beef and cook for 3–4 minutes, or until golden, breaking up the lumps with a wooden spoon. Add the tomato paste and the puréed tomato mixture, then reduce the heat and simmer for 5 minutes, or until thickened slightly. Season to taste with sea salt and freshly ground black pepper.

- Spread half the corn chips in a large deep baking dish (about 20 x 32 cm/ 8 x 12½ inches). Spoon half the beef mixture over and sprinkle with half the grated cheese. Repeat with the remaining corn chips and beef mixture, then scatter the remaining cheese over the top. Bake on the top shelf of the oven for 20–25 minutes, of until the cheese is golden and bubbling. Remove from the oven.

- To make the avocado cream, put the avocado and lemon juice in a bowl and mash with a fork. Add the sour cream, mash until smooth, then season to taste.

- Divide the nachos among serving bowls. Add a dollop of avocado cream, then a spoonful of sour cream. Sprinkle with Tabasco and serve scattered with some jalapeño chilli, spring onion and coriander.

EASY BEEF FAJITAS

preparation time 15 minutes plus 1 hour marinating
cooking time 10 minutes
serves 4

60 ml (2 fl oz/¼ cup) olive oil
3–4 garlic cloves, crushed
1–2 bird's eye chillies, thinly sliced
1 teaspoon dried oregano
1 teaspoon paprika
1 teaspoon ground cumin
1 tablespoon lime juice
1 large red onion, thinly sliced
1 red capsicum (pepper), seeded
    and thinly sliced

700 g (1 lb 9 oz) rump steak, cut into
    thin strips
8 soft flour mini tortillas
3–4 tomatoes, thinly sliced
2 avocados, thinly sliced
4 tablespoons coriander (cilantro)
    leaves
200 g (7 oz) mixed lettuce leaves,
    to serve
lime wedges, to serve

● Combine the oil, garlic, chilli, oregano, paprika, cumin, lime juice, onion and capsicum in a bowl and stir to combine well. Add the meat, toss to coat well, then cover and refrigerate for 1 hour.

● Heat a frying pan over high heat, add the steak mixture and cook, stirring, for 3–4 minutes or until the meat is cooked but still a little pink in the middle. Cook a little longer if desired.

● Place a frying pan over medium heat and when hot, add the tortillas one at a time and cook for 3 minutes or until soft and bubbles appear on the surface.

● To serve, divide the steak mixture among the tortillas and top with the tomato, avocado and coriander. Serve with lettuce leaves and lime wedges on the side.

SPICY LAMB AND CARROT OMELETTE

preparation time 10 minutes
cooking time 35 minutes
serves 4

1 tablespoon olive oil
1 onion, finely diced
300 g (10½ oz) minced (ground)
   lamb
½ teaspoon ground cumin
½ teaspoon ground cinnamon
a pinch of saffron threads

1 large carrot, roughly grated
1 handful coriander (cilantro) leaves,
   roughly chopped
1 small handful mint, roughly
   chopped, plus extra, to garnish
6 eggs, lightly beaten
yoghurt, to serve

- Preheat the oven to 160°C (315°F/Gas 2–3).

- Heat the olive oil in an 18 cm (7 inch) ovenproof non-stick frying pan over medium heat. Add the onion and sauté for 2 minutes, or until starting to soften. Add the lamb and cook for 5 minutes, or until golden, breaking up the lumps with a wooden spoon. Add the cumin, cinnamon and saffron and cook, stirring, for 1 minute, or until fragrant.

- Remove from the heat and stir the grated carrot, coriander and mint through. Return to the heat, then pour in the eggs and cook for 3 minutes, or until the edge of the omelette begins to turn golden brown. Transfer the pan to the oven and bake for 20 minutes, or until the omelette is firm to the touch.

- Cut the omelette into wedges, sprinkle with mint and serve with a spoonful of yoghurt.

Snacks & light meals

BAKED POTATOES WITH THREE TOPPINGS

preparation time 20 minutes
cooking time 1 hour
serves 4

4 large potatoes (150 g/5½ oz each),
such as king edward, sebago or
desiree

BACON, CHEESE AND CREAMED CORN TOPPING

4 slices of bacon, chopped
125 g (4½ oz) tinned creamed corn
60 g (2¼ oz/½ cup) grated cheddar
cheese
2 tablespoons finely chopped chives

RICOTTA, BABY SPINACH AND HAM TOPPING

1 tablespoon olive oil
1 small red onion, finely chopped
80 g (2¾ oz/½ cup) chopped leg ham
50 g (1¾ oz/1 cup) baby English
spinach leaves
160 g (5½ oz/⅔ cup) fresh, firm
ricotta cheese
3 spring onions (scallions),
finely sliced

CHORIZO, TOMATO AND OLIVE TOPPING

2 chorizo sausages, chopped
2 tomatoes (125 g/4½ oz), chopped
40 g (1½ oz/¼ cup) pitted kalamata
olives, chopped
2 tablespoons chopped basil
50 g (1¾ oz/⅓ cup) crumbled feta
cheese

- Preheat the oven to 200°C (400°F/Gas 6). Wash and dry the potatoes, pierce them with a fork, then wrap each one in foil. Bake for 1 hour, or until the potatoes 'give' when gently squeezed.

- Just before the potatoes are cooked, prepare your desired toppings.

- For the bacon, cheese and creamed corn topping, cook the bacon in a non-stick frying pan over medium heat for 3 minutes, or until crisp. Remove from the heat and drain on paper towels. Meanwhile, heat the creamed corn in a small saucepan until warmed through. Transfer to a bowl, stir in the bacon and cheese and sprinkle with the chives.

- For the ricotta, baby spinach and ham topping, heat the olive oil in a small frying pan over medium heat, add the onion and cook for 2 minutes, or until softened. Remove from the heat and place in a large bowl. Add the chopped ham, spinach and ricotta and mix well. Sprinkle with the spring onion.

- For the chorizo, tomato and olive topping, place the chorizo in a small frying pan over medium heat and cook for 5 minutes, stirring often, until golden. Add the tomatoes and olives and cook for 2 minutes, or until the tomatoes start to soften. Transfer to a bowl and sprinkle with the basil and feta.

- When the potatoes are ready, remove them from the oven, remove the foil and cut a cross into the top of each potato. Squeeze them around the middle with your fingers to push open the potatoes. Serve with your choice of topping.

SOUFFLE OMELETTE WITH HAM AND GRUYERE CHEESE

preparation time 10 minutes
cooking time 10 minutes
makes 1

50 g (1¾ oz) smoked ham
   (about 1 thin slice), chopped
1 teaspoon dijon mustard
2 eggs, separated
1 tablespoon cream
½ tablespoon butter
35 g (1¼ oz/¼ cup) grated
   gruyère cheese

TOMATO SALAD
1 small roma (plum) tomato, chopped
2 semi-dried tomatoes, chopped
1 tablespoon finely chopped flat-leaf
   (Italian) parsley
pinch caster (superfine) sugar
1 tablespoon extra virgin olive oil

● Combine the ham and mustard in a small bowl, then mix to coat the ham.
Set aside.

● Place the egg yolks and cream in a small bowl and whisk until combined,
then season to taste with sea salt and freshly ground black pepper. Place the
egg whites in a clean bowl and whisk until soft peaks form. Fold the egg whites
into the yolk mixture.

- Place a small non-stick frying pan over medium–low heat, add the butter, then heat until foaming. Add the egg mixture, spreading it to evenly cover the pan, then cook for 2 minutes or until the edges are set. Scatter the ham over, then sprinkle with the cheese. Cook for 2 minutes or until the omelette is puffy and the cheese is starting to melt. Fold the omelette over using a spatula and cook for 2 minutes more. Remove from the heat, then stand for 2 minutes.

- To make the tomato salad, combine all the ingredients in a small bowl and toss until well combined.

- Place the omelette on a plate, top with the salad and serve immediately.

BACON AND SPINACH BAKE WITH TOMATO, OLIVE AND CAPER RELISH

preparation time 30 minutes

cooking time 45 minutes

serves 4

40 g (1½ oz/¼ cup) sesame seeds

250 g (9 oz) bacon, cut into 1 cm
(½ inch) pieces

240 g (6 oz/3 cups) fresh mixed-grain
breadcrumbs

150 ml (5 fl oz) cream

165 g (5¾ oz/1⅓ cups) grated
gruyère cheese

3 eggs, lightly beaten

1 small handful flat-leaf (Italian)
parsley, chopped

1 large handful baby English
spinach leaves, finely chopped

TOMATO, OLIVE AND CAPER RELISH

1 tablespoon olive oil

1 onion, finely chopped

1 small carrot, finely chopped

1 garlic clove, finely chopped

2 teaspoons tomato paste
(concentrated purée)

400 g (14 oz) tinned chopped
tomatoes

1½ teaspoons caster (superfine)
sugar, or to taste

2 teaspoons balsamic vinegar, to taste

a pinch of chilli flakes

2 tablespoons chopped pitted green
olives

1 tablespoon capers, rinsed and
drained

2−3 tablespoons chopped basil

- Preheat the oven to 180°C (350°F/Gas 4). Grease a 14 x 24 cm (5½ x 9½ inch) baking dish and scatter with half the sesame seeds.

- Heat a non-stick frying pan over medium–high heat. Add the bacon and cook for 3–4 minutes, or until light golden and cooked through, stirring often. Remove from the heat.

- Put the breadcrumbs, cream, cheese and eggs in a large bowl and stir well with a fork. Mix the bacon, parsley and spinach through. Season to taste with sea salt and freshly ground black pepper and stir to combine well. Pour the mixture into the prepared baking dish, smoothing the surface. Sprinkle with the remaining sesame seeds. Bake for 40 minutes, or until golden and firm.

- Meanwhile, make the relish. Heat the oil in a saucepan over medium heat. Add the onion, carrot and garlic and sauté for 5–6 minutes, or until softened. Add the tomato paste and cook, stirring, for 1 minute, then add the tomatoes, sugar and vinegar and stir to combine. Bring to a simmer, reduce the heat to low and cook, stirring occasionally, for 15–20 minutes, or until reduced slightly. Season to taste and keep warm. Just before serving, stir in the chilli flakes, olives, capers and basil.

- Cut the bacon and spinach bake into slices and serve with the relish.

BAKED SPANISH OMELETTE

preparation time 15 minutes plus 1 hour soaking if using saffron
cooking time 30 minutes
serves 4

a large pinch of saffron threads
   (optional)
60 ml (2 fl oz/¼ cup) olive oil
1 desiree potato, peeled and cut
   into 1 cm (½ inch) chunks
1 onion, finely chopped
2 garlic cloves, crushed

115 g (4 oz/¾ cup) chopped leg ham
185 g (6½ oz/1 cup) peeled broad
   (fava) beans
6 large eggs, lightly beaten
1 small handful flat-leaf (Italian)
   parsley, finely chopped

● If using the saffron, put it in a small cup with 1 tablespoon hot water. Stand at room temperature for 1 hour to infuse.

● Preheat the oven to 200°C (400°F/Gas 6). Heat the olive oil in an ovenproof frying pan with an 18 cm (7 inch) base. Add the potato and cook over medium heat for 8–10 minutes, or until just tender, turning occasionally.

● Add the onion and garlic to the pan and sauté over medium–low heat for 5 minutes, or until the onion has softened. Add the ham and the broad beans and cook for 2–3 minutes, then press the vegetables down in the pan with the back of a wooden spoon until the surface is even.

● Combine the eggs and parsley in a small bowl with the saffron mixture, if using; mix well. Pour over the potato mixture and season with sea salt and freshly ground pepper. Transfer the pan to the oven and bake the omelette for 10 minutes, or until golden and set in the middle.

● Invert the omelette onto a plate. Cut into wedges and serve warm.

PORK WON TON SOUP

preparation time 25 minutes
cooking time 15 minutes
serves 4

400 g (14 oz) minced (ground) pork
200 g (7 oz) raw prawns (shrimp),
   peeled, deveined and chopped
1½ teaspoons sesame oil
1 tablespoon soy sauce, plus extra,
   to serve (optional)
1 tablespoon oyster sauce
1 tablespoon cornflour (cornstarch)
2 spring onions (scallions), sliced

250 g (9 oz) packet won ton wrappers
2 litres (70 fl oz/8 cups) chicken stock
180 g (6 oz) fresh egg noodles
3 baby bok choy (pak choy), trimmed
   and roughly chopped
100 g (3½ oz) fresh shiitake or oyster
   mushrooms, sliced
hot chilli sauce, to serve (optional)

- Put the pork, prawns, sesame oil, soy sauce, oyster sauce, cornflour and half the spring onion in a bowl. Using your hands, knead the mixture together until it feels slightly elastic. Place heaped teaspoons of the mixture on the won ton wrappers, lightly brush the edges with water, then fold up the corners of each wrapper to enclose the filling.

- Bring the stock to the boil in a large saucepan. Add the won tons in two batches and cook for 5 minutes each batch, or until they rise to the surface. Remove using a slotted spoon and divide among large warm deep bowls.

- Bring the stock back to the boil, if necessary, then add the egg noodles and cook for 1–2 minutes. Add the bok choy and mushrooms and cook for a further 1–2 minutes, or until the bok choy begins to wilt.

- Divide the hot broth, noodles and vegetables among the bowls. Sprinkle with the remaining spring onion and serve immediately, with chilli sauce and extra soy sauce, if desired.

STUFFED PRAWN OMELETTES

preparation time 25 minutes
cooking time 15 minutes
serves 8

500 g (1 lb 2 oz) raw prawns (shrimp)
1½ tablespoons oil
4 eggs, lightly beaten
2 tablespoons fish sauce
8 spring onions (scallions), chopped
6 coriander (cilantro) roots, chopped
2 garlic cloves, chopped
1 small red chilli, seeded and chopped
2 teaspoons lime juice

2 teaspoons grated palm sugar
    (jaggery) or soft brown sugar
3 tablespoons chopped coriander
    (cilantro) leaves
1 small red chilli, extra, chopped,
    to garnish
coriander (cilantro) sprigs, to garnish
sweet chilli sauce, to serve

● Peel the prawns, gently pull out the dark vein from each prawn back, starting from the head end, then chop the prawn meat.

● Heat a wok over high heat, add 2 teaspoons of the oil and swirl to coat. Combine the egg with half of the fish sauce. Add 2 tablespoons of the mixture to the wok and swirl to make a 16 cm (6¼ inch) round. Cook for 1 minute, then gently lift out. Repeat with the remaining egg mixture to make eight omelettes.

● Heat the remaining oil in the wok. Add the prawns, spring onion, coriander root, garlic and chilli. Stir-fry for 3–4 minutes, or until the prawns are cooked. Stir in the lime juice, palm sugar, coriander leaves and remaining fish sauce.

● Divide the prawn mixture among the omelettes and fold each into a small firm parcel. Cut a slit in the top and garnish with chilli and coriander sprigs. Serve with sweet chilli sauce.

FISH TORTILLAS WITH MANGO AND GREEN CHILLI SALSA

preparation time 15 minutes
cooking time 10 minutes
serves 4

8 soft flour tortillas
1 tablespoon olive oil
500 g (1 lb 2 oz) firm white fish fillets
(such as cod, snapper or flathead),
cut into strips 2 cm (¾ inch) thick
375 ml (13 fl oz) jar of chunky mild
salsa (available from supermarkets)

**MANGO AND GREEN CHILLI
SALSA**
1 large ripe mango, chopped
1 large green chilli, seeded and
finely chopped
1 small handful coriander (cilantro)
leaves, chopped
1 tablespoon finely chopped red
onion
½ teaspoon ground cumin
1 tablespoon olive oil
1 tablespoon lime juice

● Put all the mango salsa ingredients in a small bowl and gently mix together.
Season to taste with sea salt and freshly ground black pepper, then cover and
set aside until required.

● Heat the tortillas according to the packet instructions. Keep warm.

● Meanwhile, heat the olive oil in a large frying pan over medium heat. Cook
the fish in batches for 1 minute on each side, or until almost cooked through.
Return all the fish to the pan, add the bottled salsa and gently stir to combine.
Heat until warmed through.

● Spread the tortillas with the fish mixture and top with the mango salsa.

Snacks & light meals

BAKED SILVERBEET, TUNA AND PECORINO OMELETTE

preparation time 20 minutes
cooking time 35 minutes
serves 4

1 kg (2 lb 4 oz/1 bunch) silverbeet
   (Swiss chard), white stalks
   removed
80 ml (2½ fl oz/⅓ cup) olive oil
½ onion, finely chopped
1 garlic clove, crushed
6 large eggs
80 ml (2½ fl oz/⅓ cup) cream
425 g (15 oz) tinned tuna, drained
75 g (2½ oz/¾ cup) grated pecorino
   cheese
40 g (1½ oz/½ cup) fresh
   breadcrumbs
2 tablespoons roughly chopped
   flat-leaf (Italian) parsley

TOMATO SAFFRON SAUCE
2 tablespoons extra virgin olive oil
½ onion, finely chopped
1 garlic clove, crushed
a pinch of saffron threads
3 tomatoes (about 500 g/1 lb 2 oz
   in total), roughly chopped
2 teaspoons honey
½ teaspoon finely grated lemon rind

● Preheat the oven to 180°C (350°F/Gas 4).

● Wash the silverbeet leaves, drain well, then chop roughly. Place in a large saucepan, cover tightly and cook over medium–high heat for 4–5 minutes, or until completely wilted, shaking the pan now and then. Tip into a colander to drain and cool slightly. Squeeze the silverbeet with your hands to remove as much liquid as possible, then chop finely and set aside.

- Heat half the olive oil in a large (26 cm/ 10½ inch), deep heavy-based frying pan. Add the onion and garlic and sauté for 4 minutes, or until softened. Set aside briefly.

- In a bowl, whisk together the eggs and cream. Stir in the onion mixture from the pan, as well as the silverbeet, tuna and half the pecorino.

- Place the frying pan back over medium heat. Add the remaining oil and swirl to coat the base and side. Pour in the egg mixture and sprinkle with the breadcrumbs and remaining pecorino. Transfer the pan to the oven and bake for 25 minutes, or until set. Remove from the oven and leave to cool in the pan for 15 minutes.

- While the omelette is in the oven, make the tomato saffron sauce. Heat the olive oil in a saucepan over medium heat. Add the onion and garlic and sauté for 3 minutes, then add the saffron, tomato, honey and lemon rind and season with sea salt and freshly ground black pepper. Bring to a simmer, then cook over medium–low heat for 20–30 minutes, or until reduced and thickened.

- Carefully run a knife around the edge of the pan to loosen the omelette. Invert onto a large plate, then invert onto another plate so the crumbs are on the top. Sprinkle with the parsley, cut into wedges and serve with the saffron tomato sauce.

Rice & grains

Nutritious, filling and full of flavour and texture...what more could you ask of such useful ingredients?

TERIYAKI CHICKEN WITH RICE AND VEGETABLES

preparation time 20 minutes plus 2 hours marinating
cooking time 20 minutes
serves 4–6

800 g (1 lb 12 oz) boneless, skinless chicken thighs, trimmed and cut into strips 2 cm (¾ inch) thick
140 ml (4½ fl oz) teriyaki marinade
300 g (10½ oz/1½ cups) jasmine rice
60 ml (2 fl oz/¼ cup) vegetable oil
2 teaspoons sesame oil
1 garlic clove, crushed
1 tablespoon finely grated fresh ginger

4 spring onions (scallions), cut into long thin strips
1 carrot, cut into thin matchsticks
150 g (5½ oz) oyster mushrooms
8 baby corn, about 100 g (3½ oz)
12 snow peas (mangetout), trimmed
1 tablespoon sesame seeds

• Place the chicken in a bowl. Add the teriyaki marinade and toss to coat. Cover and refrigerate for at least 2 hours. Drain well, reserving the marinade.

• Preheat the oven to 150°C (300°F/Gas 2).

• Rinse the rice until the water runs clear. Place in a saucepan with 350 ml (12 fl oz) water. Bring to the boil and boil for 1 minute. Cover tightly, reduce the heat to as low as possible and cook for 10 minutes. Remove from the heat and leave to stand, covered, for 10 minutes.

• Meanwhile, heat a wok over high heat. Add 1 tablespoon of the vegetable oil and swirl to coat the side. Cook the chicken in batches for 4–5 minutes each batch, or until light golden and just cooked through, turning often.

- Put the chicken in a baking dish. Cover with foil and keep warm in the oven.

- Heat the sesame oil and remaining vegetable oil in the wok. Add the garlic, ginger, spring onion, carrot, mushrooms, baby corn and snow peas and stir-fry for 2–3 minutes, or until the vegetables are starting to soften.

- Add the chicken and the reserved marinade. Cook, tossing, for 1–2 minutes, or until the liquid boils.

- Serve the teriyaki chicken with the rice, sprinkled with the sesame seeds.

CHICKEN AND RICE WITH LEMONGRASS AND GINGER

preparation time 15 minutes plus 20 minutes marinating
cooking time 20 minutes
serves 4

6 dried shiitake mushrooms
500 g (1 lb 2 oz) boneless, skinless
   chicken thighs, trimmed and cut
   into slices 1 cm (½ inch) thick
1 lemongrass stem, white part only,
   finely chopped
1.5 cm (⅝ inch) knob of fresh ginger,
   peeled and cut into thin
   matchsticks
1 garlic clove, chopped

60 ml (2 fl oz/¼ cup) oyster sauce
2 tablespoons soy sauce, plus extra,
   to serve (optional)
1 tablespoon cornflour (cornstarch)
1½ teaspoons sesame oil
2 Chinese pork sausages (lap cheong),
   about 60 g (2¼ oz), thinly sliced
300 g (10½ oz/1½ cups) long-grain
   white rice
2 spring onions (scallions), sliced

• Put the mushrooms in a heatproof bowl and pour in enough boiling water to just cover. Leave to soak for 20 minutes, or until the mushrooms have softened. Drain well, discard the stems, then thinly slice the mushrooms.

• Place the mushrooms in a bowl with the chicken, lemongrass, ginger, garlic, oyster sauce, soy sauce, cornflour, sesame oil and Chinese sausage. Mix well with clean hands until all the ingredients are well coated.

• Wash the rice in several changes of cold water until the water runs almost clear. Place in a flameproof casserole dish with 750 ml (26 fl oz/3 cups) water. Cover, bring to the boil, then reduce the heat to a simmer. Once the rice begins to simmer, spread the chicken and sausage mixture on top of the rice. Cover and cook for 15–17 minutes, or until the liquid has been absorbed.

• Remove the rice from the heat and leave to stand, covered, for 10 minutes. Mix together well, then sprinkle with the spring onion and serve with extra soy sauce, if desired.

Rice & grains

CHICKEN RISONI WITH ORANGE AND BASIL

preparation time 15 minutes
cooking time 35 minutes
serves 4–6

20 g (¾ oz) unsalted butter

1 tablespoon olive oil

2 leeks, white part only, washed well, cut in half lengthways, then cut into 1 cm (½ inch) slices

500 g (1 lb 2 oz) chicken thigh fillets, trimmed and cut into 2 cm (¾ inch) chunks

60 ml (2 fl oz/¼ cup) white wine

500 ml (17 fl oz/2 cups) chicken stock

2 garlic cloves, finely chopped

1 tablespoon tomato paste (concentrated purée)

1 rosemary sprig

zest of ½ orange, cut into strips 1 cm (½ inch) wide, all white pith removed, plus 1 teaspoon finely grated orange rind

300 g (10½ oz/1½ cups) risoni (rice-shaped pasta)

2 zucchini (courgettes), cut into 5 mm (¼ inch) rounds

80 ml (2½ fl oz/⅓ cup) orange juice

1 handful basil leaves, torn

2 roma (plum) tomatoes, finely diced

shaved pecorino cheese, to serve

● Heat the butter and olive oil in a heavy-based saucepan over medium–low heat. Add the leek and sauté for 10 minutes, or until very soft. Remove to a plate and set aside.

● Increase the heat to medium–high, add the chicken to the pan and cook for 5 minutes, stirring occasionally.

● Return the leek to the pan, then pour in the wine and cook for 1 minute, or until the liquid has reduced by half. Add the stock, garlic, tomato paste, rosemary sprig and orange zest and bring to the boil. Reduce the heat to medium and simmer for 7–8 minutes, or until the chicken is nearly tender. Season to taste with sea salt and freshly ground black pepper.

● Stir in the risoni and 250 ml (9 fl oz/1 cup) boiling water, adding extra boiling water if necessary to cover all the ingredients. Cover and simmer for 6 minutes, then add the zucchini and cook for another 2–3 minutes, or until the risoni and zucchini are just tender. The mixture should be a little sloppy.

● Discard the rosemary sprig and orange zest. Stir in the grated orange rind, orange juice, basil and tomato. Divide among warm deep bowls, scatter with shaved pecorino and serve.

CHICKEN WITH GREEN RICE AND CORN

preparation time 20 minutes
cooking time 45 minutes
serves 4–6

60 ml (2 fl oz/¼ cup) extra virgin
   olive oil
2 onions, finely chopped
1 green capsicum (pepper), finely
   chopped
2 garlic cloves, finely chopped
1½ teaspoons cumin seeds
2 teaspoons dried oregano
8 chicken drumsticks, skin left on,
   knuckle end trimmed (ask your
   butcher to do this)

300 g (10½ oz/1½ cups) long-grain
   white rice
375 ml (13 fl oz/1½ cups) chicken
   stock or water
420 g (15 oz) tin corn kernels,
   drained
lime wedges, to serve

SPICE PASTE
1 large green chilli, roughly chopped
150 g (5½ oz/3⅓ cups) baby English
   spinach leaves
1 large handful coriander (cilantro),
   roughly chopped
1 small handful flat-leaf (Italian)
   parsley, roughly chopped
finely grated rind and juice of 1 lime

• Preheat the oven to 180°C (350°F/Gas 4).

• Heat the oil in a large flameproof casserole dish over medium heat. Add the onion, capsicum and garlic and sauté for 6–7 minutes, or until softened. Stir in the cumin seeds and oregano until well combined, then transfer the mixture to a bowl.

• Add the chicken to the pan, in batches if necessary, and season with sea salt and freshly ground black pepper. Cook, turning often, for 3–4 minutes, or until sealed all over. Add the rice, stock, corn and the onion mixture to the pan. Stir together well, then bring to the boil. Cover, transfer to the oven and bake for 25 minutes, or until the rice is nearly tender and the liquid is mostly absorbed.

• Meanwhile, put the spice paste ingredients in a food processor and blend until a coarse paste forms. Stir the spice paste through the rice, then cover and bake for another 5 minutes, or until the mixture is heated through and the rice is tender. Serve with lime wedges.

Rice & grains

BAKED CHICKEN, PROSCIUTTO AND PEA RISOTTO

preparation time 30 minutes
cooking time 40 minutes
serves 4

2 tablespoons olive oil
20 g (¾ oz) butter
1 large onion, finely chopped
2 garlic cloves, crushed
2 teaspoons thyme leaves, chopped
275 g (9¾ oz/1¼ cups) arborio rice
1.5 litres (52 fl oz/6 cups) chicken
  stock
2 x 150 g (5½ oz) boneless, skinless
  chicken breasts, cut into 5 mm
  (¼ inch) slices

155 g (5½ oz/1 cup) frozen peas,
  thawed
100 g (3½ oz) prosciutto, torn into
  3 cm (1¼ inch) strips
25 g (1 oz/¼ cup) finely grated
  parmesan cheese
1 small handful flat-leaf (Italian)
  parsley, chopped

● Preheat the oven to 180°C (350°F/Gas 4).

● Heat the oil and butter in a large flameproof casserole dish over medium
heat until the butter has melted. Sauté the onion and garlic for 5 minutes,
or until the onion is lightly golden.

● Add the thyme and rice and cook, stirring, for 1 minute, or until the rice is
coated with the butter mixture. Pour in the stock, then bring to the boil over
high heat, stirring continuously. Cover and bake for 15 minutes.

• Stir in the chicken and peas, then cover and bake for another 15 minutes, or until the chicken is cooked through and the rice and peas are tender. Gently stir in the prosciutto, parmesan and parsley and serve immediately.

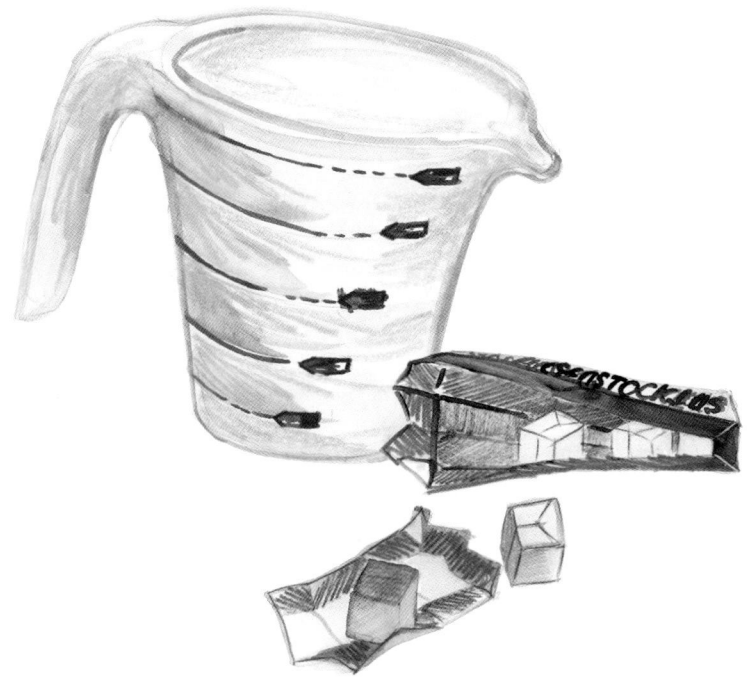

MUSHROOM AND CHICKEN RISOTTO WITH OLIVE AND HERB SPRINKLE

preparation time 20 minutes
cooking time 40 minutes
serves 4

1.125 litres (40 fl oz/4½ cups)
   chicken stock
1 tablespoon olive oil
20 g (¾ oz) butter
2 leeks, white part only, finely sliced
1 garlic clove, crushed
400 g (14 oz/4½ cups) sliced Swiss
   brown mushrooms
330 g (11½ oz/1½ cups) arborio rice
2 small boneless, skinless chicken
   breasts (about 350 g/12 oz), diced
1 large handful baby English
   spinach leaves
65 g (2¼ oz/⅔ cup) finely grated
   parmesan cheese, plus shaved
   parmesan cheese, to serve

OLIVE AND HERB SPRINKLE
110 g (3¾ oz/½ cup) green olives,
   pitted and finely sliced
1 small handful basil, torn
1 small handful flat-leaf (Italian)
   parsley, torn
1 tablespoon grated lemon rind

● Put all the ingredients for the olive and herb sprinkle in a small bowl. Mix together and set aside until ready to serve.

● Bring the stock to the boil in a saucepan, then keep hot over low heat.

● Heat the olive oil and butter in a large heavy-based saucepan over medium heat. Sauté the leek and garlic for 2 minutes, or until the leek has softened. Add the mushrooms and cook for a further 2 minutes, or until softened.

• Add the rice and stir using a wooden spoon until the grains are well coated. Stir in a ladleful of the hot stock to the rice and stir until the liquid has been completely absorbed. Continue to add the stock, one ladleful at a time, stirring constantly until the rice absorbs the stock before adding more. Add the chicken with the last ladlefuls of stock and cook for 5 minutes, until the rice is al dente and creamy and the chicken is cooked through.

• Stir in the spinach and grated parmesan and divide among serving bowls. Serve scattered with the shaved parmesan and the olive and herb sprinkle.

BEEF KOFTAS WITH RAISIN, DILL AND CARROT PILAFF

preparation time 15 minutes
cooking time 30 minutes
serves 4

PILAFF
400 g (14 oz/2 cups) long-grain
   white rice
60 g (2¼ oz) unsalted butter
1 tablespoon olive oil
2 carrots, finely diced
1 teaspoon dill seeds
30 g (1 oz/¼ cup) raisins
250 ml (9 fl oz/1 cup) chicken stock

BEEF KOFTAS
750 g (1 lb 10 oz) minced (ground)
   beef
1 slice of stale bread, torn into chunks
½ teaspoon ground allspice
1 teaspoon ground cumin
1 garlic clove, chopped
1 small onion, diced
1 handful flat-leaf (Italian) parsley
½ teaspoon salt
250 ml (9 fl oz/1 cup) tomato passata
   (puréed tomatoes)

- Preheat the oven to 180°C (350°F/Gas 4).

- To make the pilaff, wash the rice under cold water until the water runs clear, then drain well in a colander and set aside.

- Heat the butter and oil in a flameproof casserole dish over medium heat. Add the diced carrot, stir to coat in the butter, then sauté for 5 minutes. Add the dill seeds and rice, stirring for a minute or until the rice is transparent. Scatter the raisins over the top, pour in the stock and 625 ml (21½ fl oz/2½ cups) water, then cover and bring to the boil. Transfer to the oven and cook for 20 minutes. Remove from the oven, leave the lid on and leave to stand in a warm place.

• Meanwhile, make the beef koftas. Put the beef, bread, spices, garlic, onion, parsley and salt in a food processor, season with freshly ground black pepper and blend until well combined. With moistened hands, roll heaped tablespoons of the kofta mixture into about 16 balls. Place in a baking dish large enough to comfortably fit the koftas in a single layer. Mix the tomato passata with 250 ml (9 fl oz/1 cup) boiling water and pour over the meatballs. Cover with foil and bake for 15 minutes, or until the meatballs are cooked through.

• Stir the raisins through the pilaff to mix well, then spoon a mound of rice onto serving plates. Top with the meatballs, spoon the juices from the baking dish over the top and serve.

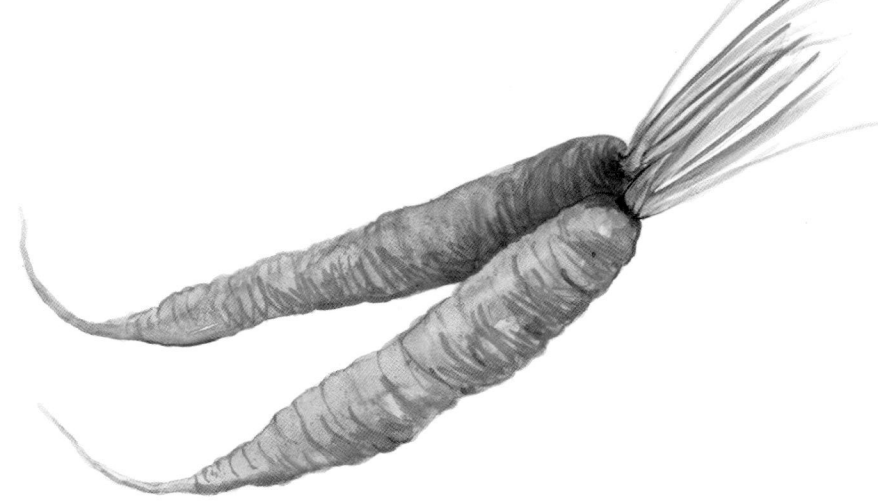

LAMB MEATBALLS WITH COUSCOUS

preparation time 30 minutes
cooking time 40 minutes
serves 4

1 tablespoon vegetable oil
½ large onion, finely chopped
1 garlic clove, crushed
½ teaspoon ground cumin
¾ teaspoon ground cinnamon
a pinch of saffron
2 tablespoons honey
125 g (4½ oz/⅔ cup) pitted
   dates, chopped
2 tablespoons tomato paste
   (concentrated purée)
400 g (14 oz) tin chopped tomatoes
375 g (13 oz/2 cups) instant couscous
20 g (¾ oz) butter
1 tablespoon olive oil
chopped coriander (cilantro) leaves,
   to serve

LAMB MEATBALLS
500 g (1 lb 2 oz) minced (ground)
   lamb
½ large onion, finely diced
1 garlic clove, crushed
1 tablespoon fennel seeds
½ teaspoon ground cumin
¼ teaspoon ground cinnamon
2 tablespoons tomato paste
   (concentrated purée)
1 small handful coriander (cilantro)
   leaves, chopped
1 small handful chopped flat-leaf
   (Italian) parsley

• Put all the ingredients for the lamb meatballs in a bowl. Season with sea salt and freshly ground black pepper and mix together well. Take heaped teaspoons of the mixture and roll them into little balls, then set aside.

• Heat the oil in a flameproof casserole dish or large frying pan over medium heat. Sauté the onion and garlic for 2 minutes. Stir in the cumin, cinnamon, saffron, honey, dates, tomato paste and tomatoes and bring to a simmer, then cook over medium–low heat for 5 minutes.

● Gently place the meatballs in the tomato sauce, then cover and cook over low heat for 30 minutes, or until the meatballs are firm and cooked through, stirring occasionally.

● Meanwhile, put the couscous in a heatproof bowl and pour over 500 ml (17 fl oz/2 cups) boiling water. Add the butter and olive oil, season well, then fluff up the grains with a fork. Cover with plastic wrap and leave to stand for 5 minutes, then fluff up the grains with a fork again to break up any lumps.

● Divide the couscous among bowls, top with the meatballs and sauce and serve sprinkled with coriander.

LAMB CUTLETS WITH SPICY RED LENTILS

preparation time 15 minutes
cooking time 25 minutes
serves 4

2 tablespoons vegetable oil, plus
    extra, for brushing
1 onion, finely chopped
1 garlic clove, finely chopped
2 cm (¾ inch) piece of fresh ginger,
    peeled and finely chopped
1 teaspoon ground cumin
1 teaspoon curry powder
½ teaspoon ground turmeric

1 teaspoon sea salt
400 g (14 oz) red lentils
3 tomatoes, diced
1 tablespoon lemon juice
300 g (10½ oz/2 cups) fresh shelled
    peas or frozen peas
8 French-trimmed lamb cutlets
40 g (1½ oz) butter
1 small handful mint leaves

● Heat the oil in a saucepan over medium heat. Add the onion and sauté for
5 minutes, or until softened. Add the garlic and ginger and cook for 2 minutes,
then stir in the spices, sea salt and lentils to combine. Add the tomatoes and
cook for 2 minutes. Add the lemon juice and 500 ml (17 fl oz/2 cups) water
and bring to the boil. Reduce the heat to medium–low and cook for
5–10 minutes, or until the lentils are just tender. Don't overcook the lentils
or they will break up and become mushy. Remove from the heat.

● Meanwhile, bring a saucepan of salted water to the boil. Add the peas and
simmer for 3–5 minutes, or until just cooked. Drain and rinse under cold water,
then drain again.

● Heat a chargrill pan or barbecue hotplate to high. Brush the lamb cutlets
with vegetable oil and season with sea salt and freshly ground black pepper.
Cook the lamb for 2–3 minutes on each side for medium–rare, or until it is
done to your liking. Cover loosely with foil and leave to rest in a warm place
for 10 minutes.

• Melt the butter in a saucepan over medium heat. Add the drained peas and mint and cook for 1 minute to heat through and wilt the mint. Season with freshly ground black pepper.

• Spoon the lentils onto serving plates. Top each with two lamb cutlets and serve with the minted peas.

CAPSICUMS STUFFED WITH LAMB AND COUSCOUS

preparation time 20 minutes
cooking time 45 minutes
serves 6

6 x 150–180 g (5½–6 oz) red or
   yellow capsicums (peppers)
140 g (5 oz/¾ cup) instant couscous
2½ tablespoons olive oil
1 onion, grated
2 garlic cloves, chopped
1 teaspoon ground cumin
2 teaspoons ground coriander
½ teaspoon ground allspice
a large pinch of chilli flakes (optional)

1 small handful chopped flat-leaf
   (Italian) parsley
1 small handful chopped mint
1 teaspoon finely grated lemon rind
250 g (9 oz) minced (ground) lamb
65 g (2½ oz/½ cup) chopped
   pistachio nuts
500 ml (17 fl oz/2 cups) tomato
   passata (puréed tomatoes)

- Preheat the oven to 190°C (375°F/Gas 5).

- Cut the tops off the capsicums and reserve. Discard the membranes and seeds from inside the capsicums.

- Place the couscous in a large heatproof bowl. Pour 125 ml (4 fl oz/½ cup) boiling water over, then cover and leave to stand for 3–5 minutes, or until the water is absorbed. Stir in 1 tablespoon of the olive oil, using a fork to break up any lumps. Stir in the onion, garlic, spices, herbs and lemon rind. Add the lamb and pistachios, then season well with sea salt and freshly ground black pepper. Mix thoroughly, using your hands.

• Spoon the mixture into the capsicum cavities. Stand the capsicums in a baking dish in which they will all fit snugly. Place the reserved capsicum lids on top.

• Combine the tomato passata with 250 ml (9 fl oz/ 1 cup) water and pour into the baking dish, around the capsicums. Drizzle the remaining oil over the capsicums. Cover with foil and bake for 20 minutes, then remove the foil and bake for another 25 minutes, or until the filling is cooked and the capsicums are tender.

• Serve hot or at room temperature, with the passata sauce.

Rice & grains

LAMB, LEMON AND RICE SOUP

preparation time 10 minutes
cooking time 35 minutes
serves 4

3 tablespoons olive oil, plus extra,
   for drizzling
2 small onions, chopped
4 small desiree potatoes, peeled and
   cut into 1 cm (½ inch) pieces
2 garlic cloves, crushed
200 g (7 oz/1 cup) medium-grain rice
large pinch ground allspice
2 teaspoons dried mint

1.5 litres (52 fl oz/6 cups) chicken
   stock
4 handfuls baby spinach leaves
600 g (1 lb 5 oz) lamb fillets, trimmed
   and cut into 1 cm (½ inch) pieces
2 tablespoons lemon juice, or to taste
Greek-style yoghurt and lemon
   wedges, to serve

• Heat the oil in a small saucepan over medium heat. Add the onion, potato and garlic and cook, stirring, for 5 minutes or until the vegetables have started to soften. Add the rice, allspice, mint, 1.5 litres (52 fl oz/6 cups) water and the stock, then bring the mixture to a gentle boil.

• Reduce the heat to low, partially cover the pan and cook for 20 minutes or until the rice and potato are very tender. Stir in the spinach, lamb and lemon juice, season to taste with sea salt and freshly ground black pepper, then cook for 3–4 minutes until the lamb is just cooked but still a little pink in the middle.

• Serve the soup immediately in large bowls with a drizzle of olive oil and lemon wedges, and the yoghurt on the side.

Rice & grains

PANCETTA AND BLUE CHEESE RISOTTO

preparation time 20 minutes
cooking time 40 minutes
serves 4

1½ tablespoons olive oil

175 g (6 oz) piece of pancetta,
   finely chopped

¼ cabbage (about 400 g/14 oz),
   core and outer leaves removed,
   then thinly sliced

1 onion, finely chopped

1 garlic clove, crushed

300 g (10½ oz/1⅓ cups) arborio rice

125 ml (4 fl oz/½ cup) white wine

1 litre (35 fl oz/4 cups) hot chicken
   or vegetable stock, approximately

20 g (¾ oz) butter

50 g (1¾ oz) mild blue cheese,
   crumbled

1 small handful flat-leaf (Italian)
   parsley, chopped

● Heat half the olive oil in a large heavy-based saucepan over medium heat. Add the pancetta and sauté for 4 minutes, or until light golden, then add the cabbage and sauté for another 4–5 minutes, or until the cabbage has wilted. Remove the mixture to a bowl and set aside.

● Heat the remaining olive oil in the pan. Add the onion and garlic and sauté for 5 minutes, or until the onion is softened but not browned. Add the rice and stir to coat the grains in the oil, then stir in the white wine and allow to simmer until almost all the liquid has evaporated.

● Pour in 125 ml (4 fl oz/½ cup) of the hot stock and continue cooking, stirring often, until the liquid has been almost absorbed.

● Add another 125 ml (4 fl oz/½ cup) of the stock and cook, stirring often, until almost absorbed. Continue stirring the rice and adding the stock for a further 10–12 minutes, or until the stock has mostly all been absorbed and the rice is al dente. It may be necessary to add a little more stock or water — the risotto should be creamy and will take about 20 minutes to cook.

● Stir in the butter, blue cheese, cabbage mixture and half the parsley. Divide the risotto among warm bowls and serve sprinkled with the remaining parsley.

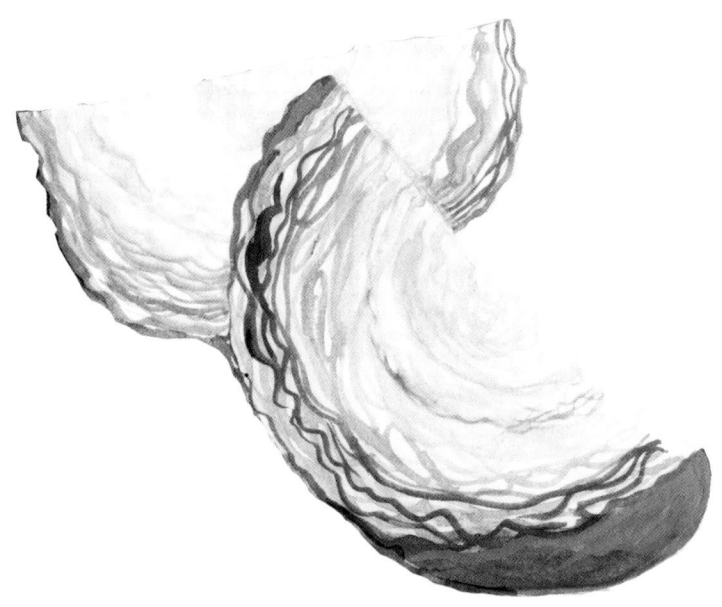

Rice & grains

PUMPKIN, BACON AND PARMESAN RISOTTO

preparation time 25 minutes
cooking time 35 minutes
serves 6

8 rindless bacon slices, about 400 g (12 oz), cut into thin strips
500 g (1 lb 2 oz) pumpkin (winter squash), cut into 1 cm (½ inch) pieces
1 thyme sprig
1.5 litres (52 fl oz/6 cups) chicken stock
2 tablespoons olive oil

2 large onions, finely chopped
2 garlic cloves, crushed
500 g (1 lb 2 oz/2¼ cups) arborio rice
250 ml (9 fl oz/1 cup) white wine
50 g (1¾ oz/½ cup) grated parmesan cheese
1 large handful flat-leaf (Italian) parsley, finely chopped

● Preheat the oven to 180°C (350°F/Gas 4).

● Line a baking tray with baking paper and add the bacon, pumpkin and thyme sprig. Season with sea salt and freshly ground black pepper and toss well. Bake for 30 minutes, or until the pumpkin is tender and the bacon is crisp. Pull the thyme leaves from the sprig and sprinkle over the pumpkin. Keep warm.

● Meanwhile, heat the chicken stock in a saucepan over medium heat. Keep at a low simmer.

● In a separate heavy-based saucepan, heat the olive oil over medium heat. Add the onion and sauté for 10 minutes, or until translucent. Add the garlic and cook for 30 seconds, then add the rice and stir to coat. Pour in the wine, bring to a simmer, then cook for 3 minutes, or until the liquid has reduced by half.

• Add 250 ml (9 fl oz/1 cup) of the hot stock to the rice mixture, then cook, stirring, until the stock has been absorbed. Continue adding the stock, 250 ml (9 fl oz/1 cup) at a time, stirring until the stock has all been used and the rice is creamy and cooked, but still a little firm. (This should take about 20 minutes; do not overcook the rice as it will continue cooking upon standing.)

• Remove the saucepan from the heat. Add the parmesan and stir to combine, then cover and leave to stand for 5 minutes.

• Stir the pumpkin, bacon and parsley into the risotto. Season to taste and serve immediately.

PORK AND CHINESE SAUSAGE STIR-FRY

preparation time 20 minutes plus 2 hours marinating
cooking time 20 minutes
serves 6

500 g (1 lb 2 oz) pork fillet, trimmed
   and thinly sliced
400 g (14 oz/2 cups) jasmine rice
1 tablespoon peanut oil
2 Chinese sausages (lap cheong),
   thinly sliced on the diagonal
200 g (7 oz/3⅓ cups) broccoli florets
1 large red capsicum (pepper), sliced
4 spring onions (scallions), shredded,
   plus extra, to garnish
200 g (7 oz) enoki mushrooms

TAMARI GARLIC MARINADE
½ teaspoon bicarbonate of soda
   (baking soda)
1 teaspoon cornflour (cornstarch)
3 tablespoons chicken stock
2 tablespoons tamari
1½ tablespoons Chinese chilli garlic
   sauce
1 tablespoon Chinese rice wine
2 teaspoons soft brown sugar
2 garlic cloves, crushed

● Combine the tamari garlic marinade ingredients in a large ceramic, glass or stainless steel bowl. Add the pork slices and toss until well coated. Cover and refrigerate for 2 hours.

● Put the rice in a saucepan with a pinch of sea salt. Add 625 ml (21½ fl oz/ 2½ cups) water. Bring to a simmer, then cover tightly and cook over low heat for 12 minutes. Leaving the lid on, remove the rice from the heat and leave to stand for 10 minutes.

● Meanwhile, drain the pork, reserving the marinade. Heat the peanut oil in a wok over high heat. Add the pork in two batches and stir-fry for 1–2 minutes, or until golden. Remove to a plate and keep warm.

● Wipe the wok clean if necessary. Add the Chinese sausage and stir-fry for 2 minutes, or until golden. Add the broccoli florets and sliced capsicum and stir-fry for 1 minute. Add 2 tablespoons water and cover with a lid to steam the vegetables for 1 minute. Add the spring onion and mushrooms and stir-fry for 1–2 minutes.

● Pour in the reserved tamari garlic marinade and return the pork to the wok. Bring to a simmer and cook for 1–2 minutes to heat through.

● Divide the rice among four serving bowls. Top with the stir-fry mixture, garnish with extra shredded spring onion and serve.

CHINESE ROAST PORK WITH ORANGE SAUCE

preparation time 15 minutes plus 1 hour marinating
cooking time 30 minutes
serves 2

2 tablespoons hoisin sauce
2 tablespoons soft brown sugar
1 tablespoon Chinese rice wine
125 ml (4 fl oz/½ cup) orange juice
2 garlic cloves, crushed
2 teaspoons sesame oil
1 star anise
3 teaspoons soy sauce

500 g (1 lb 2 oz) pork fillet (about
    1 large), trimmed
2 teaspoons peanut oil
2 teaspoons fresh ginger, cut
    into matchsticks
2 spring onions (scallions), trimmed
    and thinly sliced
½ teaspoon cornflour (cornstarch)
steamed rice, to serve
steamed bok choy (pak choy) and
    snow peas (mangetout), to serve

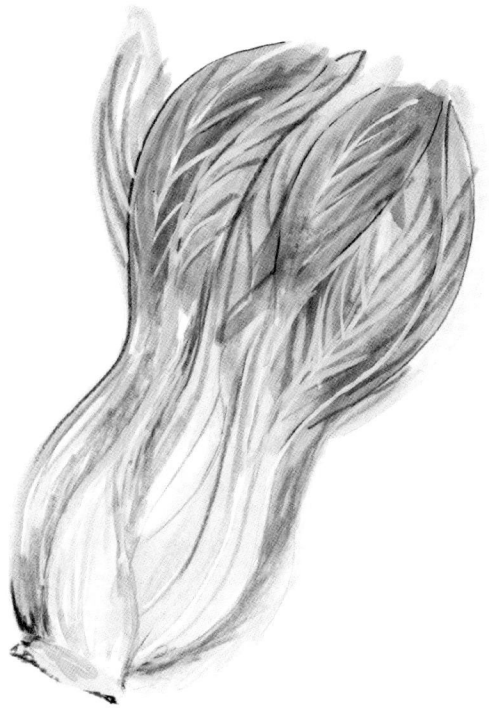

- Combine the hoisin sauce, sugar, rice wine, orange juice, garlic, sesame oil, star anise and soy sauce in a bowl and mix well. Add the pork fillet, toss to coat, then cover and refrigerate for at least 1 hour.

- Preheat the oven to 220°C (425°F/Gas 7). Drain the pork well, reserving the marinade, then place the pork on a wire rack over a roasting tin filled with 3 cm (1¼ inches) water. Roast the pork for 25 minutes or until just cooked through, brushing occasionally with some of the reserved marinade. Transfer the pork to a warm plate, cover loosely with foil and rest for 10 minutes.

- Heat the peanut oil in a small pan over low heat. Add the ginger and spring onion and cook, stirring, for 1 minute or until fragrant. Add the reserved pork marinade and bring the mixture to the boil, then cook gently for 2–3 minutes. Combine the cornflour with 2 teaspoons water to form a smooth paste. Stirring constantly, add the cornflour to the marinade and cook for 1–2 minutes or until thickened slightly. Remove the star anise and discard.

- Slice the pork on the diagonal into 1 cm (½ inch) thick pieces. Divide the rice between plates, top with the pork and steamed vegetables, spoon the sauce over and serve immediately.

Rice & grains

SPICY FISH COUSCOUS

preparation time 15 minutes
cooking time 20 minutes
serves 4–6

2 tablespoons olive oil
1 onion, chopped
2 garlic cloves, crushed
2 teaspoons Moroccan spice mix
    (available from supermarkets)
½ teaspoon chilli flakes
2 carrots, cut into 2 cm (¾ inch)
    chunks
1 red capsicum (pepper), cut into
    2 cm (¾ inch) pieces
2 zucchini (courgettes), cut into 2 cm
    (¾ inch) chunks
750 ml (26 fl oz/ 3 cups) vegetable
    stock

750 g (1 lb 10 oz) boneless thick
    white fish fillets, cut into 2 cm
    (¾ inch) cubes
425 g (15 oz/ 2¼ cups) instant
    couscous
45 g (1½ oz/⅓ cup) pistachios,
    chopped
45 g (1½ oz/¼ cup) pitted green
    olives
1 small handful flat-leaf (Italian)
    parsley
2 teaspoons chopped preserved
    lemon rind (optional)
lemon wedges, to serve
harissa, to serve

● Heat the olive oil in a large heavy-based saucepan. Add the onion, garlic, spice mix, chilli, carrot, capsicum and zucchini and sauté over low heat for 5 minutes, or until the vegetables are soft but not brown. Pour in the stock and bring to the boil, then reduce the heat, cover and simmer for 8 minutes, or until the vegetables are tender.

● Add the fish and bring the mixture back to a simmer. Season with sea salt, then gently stir in the couscous using a wooden spoon, being careful not to break up the fish. Immediately remove the pan from the heat, then cover and leave to stand for 5 minutes.

- Using a large fork, gently toss the couscous mixture to combine.

- Divide among wide shallow bowls and sprinkle with the pistachios, olives, parsley and preserved lemon, if using. Serve with lemon wedges and harissa.

FISH WITH ASPARAGUS RISOTTO AND THYME MASCARPONE

preparation time 20 minutes
cooking time 40 minutes
serves 6

80 ml (2½ fl oz/⅓ cup) olive oil

1 leek, white part only, thinly sliced

100 g (3½ oz) piece pancetta, chopped

330 g (11¾ oz/1½ cups) arborio or other risotto rice

125 ml (4 fl oz/½ cup) white wine

1.25 litres (44 fl oz/5 cups) fish or chicken stock, simmering

12–16 spears of asparagus (about 2 bunches), trimmed and cut into 3 cm (1¼ inch) pieces

20 g (¾ oz) butter, chopped

25 g (1 oz/¼ cup) grated parmesan cheese

3 teaspoons finely grated lemon rind

4 x 120 g (4¼ oz) basa, or other white fish fillets

75 g (2¾ oz/½ cup) polenta

60 g (2¼ oz/¼ cup) mascarpone cheese

1 tablespoon thyme leaves, lightly bruised

• Heat half the oil in a large saucepan over medium heat. Add the leek and pancetta and cook, stirring, for 5 minutes or until softened, then stir in the rice. Add the wine and stir until evaporated. Add 500 ml (17 fl oz/ 2 cups) hot stock. Cook, stirring frequently, for about 5–7 minutes until the liquid is absorbed.

• Add another 500 ml (17 fl oz/2 cups) hot stock and repeat the process. Add the remaining hot stock and stir in the asparagus pieces. Stir until the liquid is mostly absorbed and rice is creamy and tender. Stir in the butter, parmesan and 2 teaspoons of the lemon rind.

● Meanwhile, pat the fish fillets dry with paper towels. Put the polenta on a tray and coat the fish fillets with polenta, shaking off any excess. Heat the remaining oil in a large frying pan over medium heat. Cook the fish fillets for 3–4 minutes, turning once, or until crisp and cooked through. Drain on paper towels.

● To serve, combine the mascarpone, thyme leaves and remaining lemon rind in a small bowl. Divide the risotto among four serving plates, top each with a fish fillet and add a spoonful of thyme mascarpone. Serve immediately.

STEAMED FISH CUTLETS WITH GINGER AND CHILLI

preparation time 15 minutes
cooking time 10 minutes
serves 4

4 skinless firm white fish cutlets
     (200 g/7 oz each)
5 cm (2 inch) piece fresh ginger, cut
     into fine shreds
2 garlic cloves, chopped
2 teaspoons chopped red chilli
2 tablespoons finely chopped
     coriander (cilantro) stems
3 spring onions (scallions), cut
     into fine shreds 4 cm
     (1½ inches) long
2 tablespoons lime juice
lime wedges, to serve

● Line a bamboo steaming basket with banana leaves or baking paper (this is so the fish will not stick or taste of bamboo).

● Arrange the fish cutlets in the basket and top with the ginger, garlic, chilli and coriander. Cover and steam over a wok or large saucepan of boiling water for 5–6 minutes.

● Remove the lid and sprinkle the spring onion and lime juice over the fish. Cover and steam for 30 seconds, or until the fish is cooked. Serve immediately with wedges of lime and steamed rice.

STEAMED SNAPPER WITH BURGHUL PILAFF AND PINE NUT SAUCE

preparation time 30 minutes
cooking time 35 minutes
serves 4

4 x 150 g (5½ oz) snapper fillets,
    or other firm white fish fillets
1 teaspoon finely grated lemon rind
75 g (2½ oz/½ cup) pine nuts
½ small garlic clove, peeled
50 ml (1½ fl oz) lemon juice
50 ml (1½ fl oz) verjuice or white wine
2 teaspoons olive oil
chopped flat-leaf (Italian) parsley,
    to garnish
lemon wedges, to serve

BURGHUL PILAFF
25 g (1 oz) butter
½ onion, finely diced
½ fennel bulb, about 125 g (4½ oz),
    trimmed, cored and finely diced
½ teaspoon cumin seeds
¼ teaspoon ground allspice
¼ teaspoon chilli flakes
175 g (6 oz/1 cup) coarse burghul
    (bulgur)
375 ml (13 fl oz/1½ cups) chicken
    stock
350 ml (12 fl oz) tomato passata
    (puréed tomatoes)
40 g (1½ oz/¼ cup) currants
½ teaspoon honey
1 teaspoon pomegranate molasses
    (optional)
25 g (1 oz) flaked almonds, toasted

● To make the pilaff, melt the butter in a large saucepan over medium–low heat. Add the onion and fennel and a pinch of salt and sauté for 5 minutes, or until translucent.

● Add the spices and cook, stirring, for 30 seconds, then add the burghul, stock, passata, currants, honey and pomegranate molasses, if using. Reduce the heat to very low, cover and cook for 20–25 minutes, or until the burghul has absorbed the liquid and is tender. Remove from the heat and leave for 5 minutes. Just before serving, stir the almonds through.

● Place the fish fillets in a steamer basket, in a single layer. Sprinkle with the lemon rind and some sea salt and freshly ground black pepper. Set over a saucepan or wok of boiling water and steam for 5 minutes, or until the fish is just cooked through.

● Crush the pine nuts and garlic with a pinch of salt using a mortar and pestle or a small food processor. Mix in the lemon juice, verjuice and olive oil and stir or process until smooth, adding a teaspoon of cold water if necessary.

● Spoon the pilaff onto serving plates. Top with the fish fillets. Drizzle with the pine nut sauce, sprinkle with parsley and serve with lemon wedges.

Rice & grains

77

PRAWN AND LIME PILAFF

preparation time 25 minutes
cooking time 20 minutes
serves 4–6

300 g (10½ oz/1½ cups) jasmine rice
85 g (3 oz/1 bunch) coriander
  (cilantro)
1 tablespoon peanut or vegetable oil
4 spring onions (scallions), thinly
  sliced
1 tablespoon finely chopped fresh
  ginger
560 ml (19¼ fl oz/2¼ cups) chicken
  stock
2 tablespoons fish sauce
finely grated rind of 1 lime
1½ tablespoons lime juice

1 lemongrass stem, white part only,
  thinly sliced
150 g (5½ oz/about 1 bunch) snake
  (yard-long) beans, cut into 5 mm
  (¼ inch) lengths
300 g (10½ oz) small cleaned squid
  tubes, cut into strips measuring
  about 1 x 5 cm (½ x 2 inches)
700 g (1 lb 9 oz) raw king prawns
  (shrimp), peeled and deveined,
  then cut in half lengthways
50 g (1¾ oz/⅓ cup) cashew nuts
4 makrut (kaffir lime) leaves, finely
  shredded
lime wedges, to serve

● Put the rice in a large heavy-based saucepan and shake, uncovered, over low heat for 4 minutes, or until the rice is lightly toasted and fragrant. Transfer the rice to a plate and leave the pan to cool for a few minutes.

● Rinse the coriander bunch well, then trim and discard the roots. Finely slice the coriander stalks; shred the leaves and reserve as a garnish.

● Heat the oil in the saucepan over medium–low heat. Add the sliced coriander stalks, spring onion and ginger and sauté for 2–3 minutes, until softened. Add the rice, stock, fish sauce, lime rind, lime juice and lemongrass and bring to the boil. Cover, reduce the heat to low and simmer for 7 minutes.

● Add the snake beans, squid and prawns, then cover and cook for another 3 minutes. Without removing the lid, remove the pan from the heat and leave to stand for 5 minutes (the rice and seafood should be tender and the liquid should be absorbed).

● Divide the pilaff among warm bowls. Garnish with the cashews, lime leaves and reserved coriander leaves and serve with lime wedges.

Rice & grains

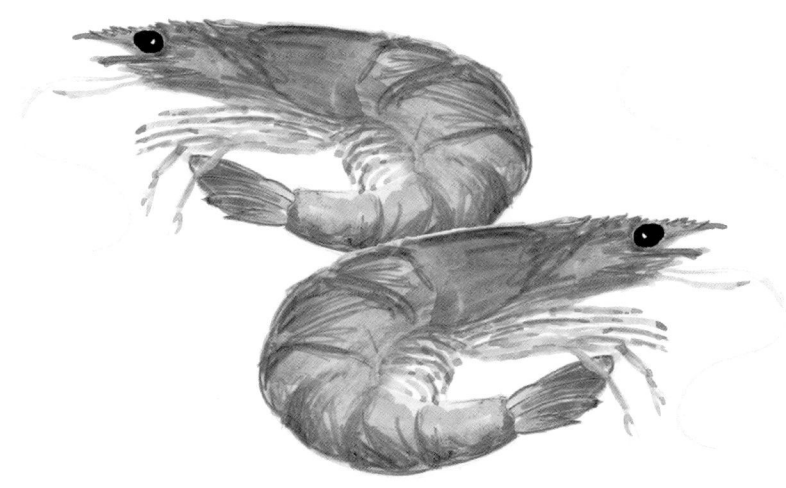

RICE BAKED WITH BEANS, SPINACH, PRAWNS AND FETA

preparation time 15 minutes

cooking time 50 minutes

serves 4

1 tablespoon olive oil

1 red onion, finely chopped

2 garlic cloves, crushed

½ teaspoon chilli flakes, or to taste

2 teaspoons thyme leaves

300 g (10½ oz/1½ cups) long-grain white rice

560 ml (19¼ fl oz/2¼ cups) vegetable or chicken stock

400 g (14 oz) tin cannellini beans, rinsed and drained

175 g (6 oz/1 cup) fresh or thawed frozen broad (fava) beans, peeled

250 g (9 oz) packet frozen chopped spinach, thawed and squeezed dry

500 g (1 lb 2 oz) raw king prawns (shrimp), peeled and deveined, tails intact

150 g (5½ oz/1 cup) crumbled feta cheese

lemon wedges, to serve

• Preheat the oven to 180°C (350°F/Gas 4).

• Heat the olive oil in a 3 litre (105 fl oz/ 12 cup) flameproof casserole dish over medium heat. Add the onion and sauté for 5 minutes, or until softened. Add the garlic, chilli and thyme and sauté for 1 minute, or until fragrant. Add the rice and stir until well coated with the oil.

• Stir in the stock and season well with freshly ground black pepper, mixing thoroughly to combine. Bring to a simmer, then cover the dish, transfer to the oven and bake for 30 minutes, or until the rice is tender and the liquid is absorbed.

• Add the cannellini beans, broad beans, spinach and prawns, pushing them into the rice so that they are covered. Scatter the feta over the top, then cover and bake for 10 minutes, or until the vegetables and prawns are cooked.

• Fluff up the rice with a fork. Serve hot, with lemon wedges.

Rice & grains

Pasta & noodles

Italian and Asian influences abound in these robust, satisfying recipes with comfort food very much in mind.

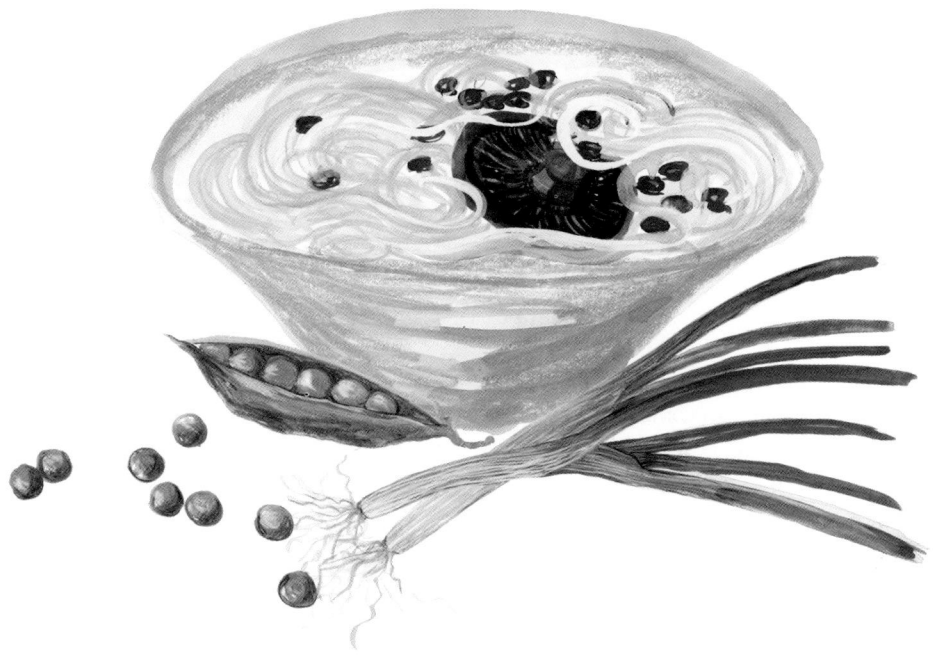

LINGUINE WITH GREEN BEANS, POTATO AND MINT AND ALMOND PESTO

preparation time 15 minutes
cooking time 20 minutes
serves 4

3 desiree or other all-purpose
    potatoes (about 400 g/14 oz),
    diced
200 g (7 oz) green beans, trimmed
    and cut into short lengths
400 g (14 oz) linguine
grated pecorino cheese, to serve
green salad, to serve

MINT AND ALMOND PESTO
60 g (2¼ oz/⅓ cup) blanched
    almonds
1 garlic clove, sliced
25 g (1 oz/1¼ cups) mint leaves,
    lightly packed
1 small handful flat-leaf (Italian)
    parsley
125 ml (4 fl oz/½ cup) extra virgin
    olive oil
50 g (1¾ oz/½ cup) grated pecorino
    cheese

• Preheat the oven to 180°C (350°F/Gas 4).

• To make the mint and almond pesto, spread the almonds on a baking tray and toast in the oven for 4–5 minutes, until lightly toasted. Allow to cool, then transfer to a food processor with the garlic and blend until finely chopped. Add the mint, parsley and olive oil, and blend until well combined. Add the pecorino and pulse until just combined. Season to taste with sea salt and freshly ground black pepper, and set aside.

• Bring a large saucepan of salted water to the boil. Add the potato and cook for 10 minutes, then add the beans and cook for a further 3 minutes, or until the vegetables are tender. Drain well.

● Meanwhile, cook the pasta in another saucepan of boiling salted water until al dente, following the packet instructions. Drain well, reserving 2 tablespoons of the cooking water.

● Return the hot pasta to the saucepan with the reserved cooking water. Add the potato, beans and mint and almond pesto, and toss until well combined.

● Divide among serving bowls. Serve scattered with extra grated pecorino, with a green salad on the side.

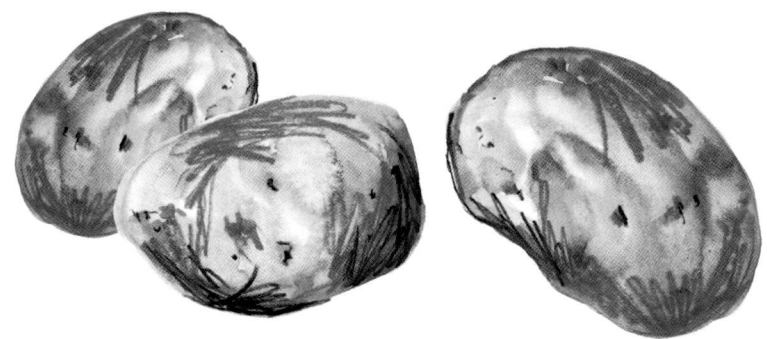

TOFU, CASHEW AND NOODLE STIR-FRY

preparation time 15 minutes
cooking time 10 minutes
serves 4

300 g (10½ oz) fresh hokkien (egg) noodles or fresh rice noodles
1 teaspoon sesame oil
2 tablespoons soy sauce
60 ml (2 fl oz/¼ cup) oyster sauce
2 tablespoons vegetable oil
1 onion, thinly sliced
2 garlic cloves, thinly sliced
200 g (7 oz/1 bunch) broccolini, stems and heads halved lengthways, then cut into 5 cm (2 inch) lengths

1 tablespoon finely grated fresh ginger
300 g (10½ oz/1 bunch) bok choy (pak choy), trimmed and cut into 5 cm (2 inch) lengths
150 g (5½ oz) firm tofu, cut into 2 cm (¾ inch) chunks
100 g (3½ oz) snow peas (mangetout), cut in half on the diagonal
50 g (1¾ oz/⅓ cup) roasted cashew nuts

- Put the noodles in a large heatproof bowl and pour in enough boiling water to cover. Leave to stand for 2–3 minutes, or until softened, then drain well.

- In a small bowl, mix together the sesame oil, soy sauce, oyster sauce and 60 ml (2 fl oz/¼ cup) water. Set aside.

- Heat the vegetable oil in a wok over high heat. Stir-fry the onion and garlic for 1 minute, then add the broccolini, ginger and bok choy and stir-fry for another minute.

- Add the drained noodles, tofu and snow peas and stir-fry for 1–2 minutes, then add the soy sauce mixture and stir-fry for another 2–3 minutes, or until the liquid boils and the vegetables are tender but still slightly crisp. Divide among warm bowls, scatter the cashews over and serve.

GNOCCHI CHEESE BAKE

preparation time 10 minutes
cooking time 15 minutes
serves 4

500 g (1 lb 2 oz) fresh potato gnocchi
30 g (1 oz) butter
1 tablespoon chopped flat-leaf
   (Italian parsley)
100 g (3½ oz) fontina cheese, sliced
100 g (3½ oz) provolone cheese,
   sliced

● Preheat the oven to 200°C (400°F/Gas 6). Cook the gnocchi, in batches, in a large saucepan of boiling water for about 2 minutes, or until the gnocchi rise to the surface. Carefully remove from the pan with a slotted spoon and drain well.

● Put the gnocchi in a lightly greased ovenproof dish. Scatter with the butter and parsley. Lay the fontina and provolone cheeses over the top of the gnocchi. Season with sea salt and cracked black pepper. Bake for 10 minutes, or until the cheese has melted.

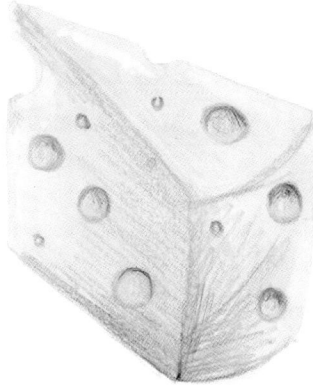

PENNE ALLA NAPOLITANA

preparation time 20 minutes
cooking time 25 minutes
serves 4–6

2 tablespoons olive oil
1 onion, finely chopped
2–3 garlic cloves, finely chopped
1 small carrot, finely diced
1 celery stalk, finely diced
800 g (1 lb 12 oz) tinned peeled,
   chopped tomatoes or 1 kg
    (2 lb 4 oz) ripe tomatoes, peeled
   and chopped

1 tablespoon tomato paste
   (concentrated purée)
3 tablespoons shredded basil
500 g (1 lb 2 oz) penne
freshly grated parmesan cheese,
   to serve (optional)

● Heat the olive oil in a large frying pan. Add the onion and garlic and cook
for 2 minutes, or until golden. Add the diced carrot and celery and cook for
a further 2 minutes.

● Add the tomato and tomato paste. Simmer for 20 minutes, or until the sauce
thickens, stirring occasionally. Stir in the shredded basil and season to taste.

● While the sauce is cooking, cook the pasta in a large saucepan of rapidly
boiling salted water until al dente. Drain well and return to the pan.

● Add the sauce to the pasta and mix well. Serve with freshly grated parmesan
cheese, if desired.

SPAGHETTINI WITH GARLIC AND CHILLI

preparation time 10 minutes
cooking time 20 minutes
serves 4–6

500 g (1 lb 2 oz) spaghettini
125 ml (4 fl oz/½ cup) extra virgin
   olive oil
2–3 garlic cloves, finely chopped
1–2 red chillies, seeded and finely
   chopped

3 tablespoons chopped flat-leaf
   (Italian) parsley
freshly grated parmesan cheese,
   to serve

- Cook the spaghettini in a large saucepan of rapidly boiling salted water until al dente. Drain and return to the pan.

- Meanwhile, heat the extra virgin olive oil in a large frying pan. Cook the garlic and chilli over very low heat for 2–3 minutes, or until the garlic is golden. Take care not to burn the garlic or chilli as this will make the sauce bitter.

- Toss the parsley and the warmed oil, garlic and chilli mixture through the pasta. Season. Serve with the parmesan.

Pasta & noodles

MEE GORENG

preparation time 10 minutes plus 10 minutes soaking
cooking time 10 minutes
serves 4–6

200 g (7 oz) dried thin egg noodles
60 ml (2 fl oz/¼ cup) vegetable oil
2 eggs, lightly beaten
2 garlic cloves, chopped
1 cm (½ inch) knob of fresh ginger,
    peeled and grated
1 carrot, cut into thin matchsticks
½ Chinese cabbage, cut into slices
    1 cm (½ inch) thick
60 ml (2 fl oz/¼ cup) soy sauce

2 tablespoons tomato sauce (ketchup)
1½ tablespoons chilli sauce, or to
    taste
8 fried tofu puffs, cut into quarters
100 g (3½ oz/1 cup) bean sprouts,
    tails trimmed
2 spring onions (scallions), sliced on
    the diagonal
sliced red chilli, to serve (optional)
lime wedges, to serve

- Put the noodles in a large heatproof bowl and cover with boiling water. Leave to soak for 10 minutes, or until the noodles are soft. Drain well.

- Heat 1 tablespoon of the oil in a wok over medium—high heat. Add half the egg and swirl the wok to spread it as thinly as possible. Cook for 1 minute, or until the egg has set and is golden underneath. Remove to a plate, then repeat with the remaining egg. Allow the omelettes to cool, then roll each one into a cylinder and slice thinly.

- Reheat the wok over medium—high heat. Pour in the remaining oil. When the oil is hot, add the garlic, ginger, carrot and cabbage and stir-fry for 1 minute. Add the noodles and cook, tossing well, for another minute.

- Add the soy sauce, tomato sauce and chilli sauce, tossing and cooking for another minute, or until the noodles are well coated and heated through. Add the omelette strips, tofu, bean sprouts and spring onion and toss to combine.

- Sprinkle with sliced chilli, if desired, and serve with lime wedges.

Pasta & noodles

SATAY CHICKEN NOODLES

preparation time 15 minutes
cooking time 15 minutes
serves 4

250 g (9 oz) fresh rice noodles
400 ml (14 fl oz) tin coconut milk
60 g (2¼ oz/¼ cup) crunchy peanut
    butter
2 teaspoons soft brown sugar
1 tablespoon lime juice
2 tablespoons fish sauce
2 tablespoons peanut oil
500 g (1 lb 2 oz) boneless, skinless
    chicken breasts, thinly sliced on
    the diagonal

60 g (2¼ oz/¼ cup) Thai Penang
    curry paste
2 garlic cloves, chopped
1 red capsicum (pepper), thinly sliced
150 g (5½ oz) snow peas (mangetout),
    trimmed and cut on the diagonal
2 kaffir lime leaves, finely shredded
2 tablespoons coriander (cilantro)
    leaves
40 g (1½ oz/¼ cup) unsalted roasted
    peanuts, chopped

• Put the noodles in a large heatproof bowl. Pour in enough boiling water to cover, then leave to soak for 3 minutes, or until soft. Drain well and set aside.

• Meanwhile, put the coconut milk, peanut butter, sugar, lime juice and fish sauce in a small food processor. Blend until a smooth paste forms. Set aside.

• Heat 1½ tablespoons of the oil in a large wok over high heat. Stir-fry the chicken, curry paste and garlic in two batches for 2 minutes each batch, or until the chicken is nearly cooked, removing each batch to a plate.

• Reheat the wok, add the remaining oil and stir-fry the capsicum over medium–high heat for 2 minutes, or until softened slightly.

• Add the peanut butter mixture to the wok and bring to a simmer. Return the chicken mixture to the wok, along with the snow peas. Toss for 1–2 minutes to heat the chicken through and soften the snow peas slightly.

• Add the noodles and toss for another 1–2 minutes to heat through. Divide the mixture among warm bowls, scatter the lime leaves, coriander and peanuts over each and serve.

Pasta & noodles

93

CHINESE-STYLE TURKEY STIR-FRY

preparation time 20 minutes
cooking time 10 minutes
serves 6

25 g (1 oz/1 cup) dried sliced shiitake
   mushrooms
100 g (3½ oz) dried bean thread
   noodles
1 teaspoon cornflour (cornstarch)
2 tablespoons oyster sauce
1 tablespoon Chinese chilli garlic
   sauce
1 tablespoon Chinese rice wine
2 teaspoons tomato sauce (ketchup)
1½ tablespoons peanut oil
1 carrot, cut into fine matchsticks
250 g (9 oz) green beans, trimmed
   and thinly sliced on the diagonal

4 spring onions (scallions), thinly
   sliced on the diagonal
1 tablespoon finely grated fresh
   ginger
400 g (14 oz) minced (ground) turkey
300 g (10½ oz) Chinese cabbage,
   shredded
1 tablespoon soy sauce
150 g (5½ oz/1⅔ cups) bean sprouts,
   trimmed
1 large handful coriander (cilantro)
   leaves

- Soak the shiitake mushrooms in a bowl of warm water for 20 minutes, or until softened. Drain well. Remove and discard the mushroom stalks, then thinly slice the caps.

- Meanwhile, soak the noodles in cold water for 15 minutes, then drain well.

- In a small bowl, mix the cornflour with 1 tablespoon cold water until smooth. Add the oyster sauce, chilli garlic sauce, rice wine and tomato sauce. Set aside.

• Heat half the peanut oil in a wok over high heat. Add the carrot, beans, spring onion and mushrooms and stir-fry for 2–3 minutes, or until softened. Remove from the wok and set aside.

• Add the remaining oil to the wok. Add the ginger and turkey and stir-fry for 3 minutes, breaking up any lumps with a fork.

• Return the vegetables to the wok and add the cabbage and noodles. Stir-fry for 1–2 minutes, or until the cabbage has wilted.

• Add the oyster sauce mixture to the stir-fry and cook until heated through. Remove from the heat, add the soy sauce, bean sprouts and coriander and toss to combine. Serve immediately.

ORECCHIETTE WITH CHICKEN SAUSAGE, TOMATO, ROCKET AND PARMESAN

preparation time 10 minutes
cooking time 20 minutes
serves 4

360 g (12¾ oz) orecchiette pasta
3 tablespoons extra virgin olive oil
600 g (1 lb 5 oz) chicken sausages,
    skins removed
2 garlic cloves, crushed
8 anchovy fillets, chopped
large pinch chilli flakes (optional)
200 ml (7 fl oz) white wine
500 g (1 lb 2 oz) cherry tomatoes,
    halved
80 ml (2½ fl oz/⅓ cup) cream
4 handfuls rocket (arugula)
shaved parmesan, to serve

- Bring a large saucepan of salted water to the boil. Add the orecchiette and cook according to packet instructions or until al dente. Drain and set aside.

- Place the oil in a heavy-based frying pan over medium–high heat. Add the sausage meat and cook for 1–2 minutes, stirring to break the meat up. Reduce the heat to low, add the garlic, anchovies and chilli, if using, and cook, stirring, for 1 minute or until the anchovies have melted. Pour in the white wine and cook until it has reduced by half. Add the tomatoes and cook for 5 minutes, or until collapsing. Add the cream and rocket and cook for 1 minute, or until the cream is heated through and the rocket is wilted. Season to taste with sea salt and freshly ground black pepper.

- Add the cooked orecchiette to the sauce and toss to combine well. Spoon into a serving bowl, top with the parmesan and serve immediately.

Pasta & noodles

CHILLI, CHICKEN AND CASHEW STIR-FRY

preparation time 15 minutes
cooking time 5 minutes
serves 4

8 small boneless, skinless chicken
   thighs, sliced
1 tablespoon cornflour (cornstarch)
2 tablespoons soy sauce
2 tablespoons oyster sauce
1–2 red bird's eye chillies, to taste,
   chopped
2 garlic cloves, chopped
1 teaspoon grated fresh ginger
2 tablespoons vegetable or peanut oil
1 red capsicum (pepper), trimmed,
   seeded and thinly sliced

2 carrots, cut in half lengthways,
   then thinly sliced
8 spring onions (scallions), trimmed
   well and cut into 5 cm (2 inch)
   lengths
2 tablespoons Chinese rice wine or
   sherry
50 g (1¾ oz/⅓ cup) roasted cashew
   nuts
1 teaspoon sesame oil (optional)
steamed rice, to serve

- Combine the chicken, cornflour, soy sauce, oyster sauce, chilli, garlic and ginger in a small bowl, tossing to coat the chicken well. Cover and refrigerate for at least 30 minutes (chicken can be marinated up to 12 hours in advance).

- Heat the oil in a wok or frying pan over medium–high heat, then add the chicken mixture and stir-fry for 1 minute. Add the capsicum, carrot and spring onion and stir-fry for 1 minute or until the vegetables begin to soften and the chicken is browned.

- Add the rice wine, cashew nuts and sesame oil, if using, and toss to combine well. Remove from the heat and serve immediately with the steamed rice.

CHICKEN RAVIOLI WITH LEMON BURNT BUTTER

preparation time 25 minutes
cooking time 10 minutes
serves 4

400 g (14 oz) minced (ground) chicken
50 g (1¾ oz/⅓ cup) currants
50 g (1¾ oz/⅓ cup) toasted pine nuts, plus extra, to serve
8–10 anchovy fillets, finely chopped
4 tablespoons finely chopped parsley
1 tablespoon finely chopped rosemary

1 tablespoon finely chopped oregano, plus a few leaves extra, to serve
32 won ton wrappers

LEMON BURNT BUTTER
60 g (2¼ oz) butter
1 lemon, zested
1–2 tablespoons lemon juice

● Combine the chicken, currants, pine nuts, anchovies and herbs in a bowl and season with sea salt and freshly ground black pepper. Stir to mix well. Lay half the won ton wrappers on a baking paper-lined baking tray, then place about 1 tablespoon of the filling onto the centre of each wrapper, flattening slightly. Lightly brush the edges of each wrapper with water to dampen slightly, then top with the remaining wrappers, lightly pressing the edges to seal.

● To make the lemon burnt butter, melt the butter in a small saucepan over medium–low heat, then cook for about 1 minute or until the butter and its solids begin to turn golden brown. Remove from the heat and add the lemon zest and juice.

● Bring a large saucepan of water to the boil, add the ravioli and cook for 5 minutes or until cooked through. Drain well. To serve, place the ravioli on a serving plate, drizzle with the lemon burnt butter, sprinkle with the extra pine nuts and oregano leaves, and serve immediately.

Pasta & noodles

BEEF AND CASHEW NOODLE SALAD

preparation time 10 minutes
cooking time 10 minutes
serves 2

750 ml (25 fl oz/3 cups) beef stock

2½ tablespoons soy sauce

2½ tablespoons lime juice

250 g (9 oz) beef eye fillet

100 g (3 oz) dried rice vermicelli
    noodles

2 tablespoons coriander (cilantro)
    leaves

1 tablespoon small mint leaves

⅓ long red chilli, seeded and thinly
    sliced lengthways

1 spring onion (scallion), trimmed and
    thinly sliced on an angle

1 small carrot, grated

½ Lebanese (short) cucumber, seeded
    and cut into fine matchsticks

1 tablespoon roasted cashews,
    coarsely chopped

DRESSING

2 tablespoons lime juice

2 tablespoons fish sauce

2 tablespoons grated palm sugar
    (jaggery)

2½ teaspoons finely grated
    fresh ginger

- To make the dressing, combine the ingredients in a small bowl and set aside.

- Put the stock, soy sauce and lime juice into a saucepan and bring to the boil over medium heat, then add the beef. Reduce the heat to low and cook gently for 5 minutes; do not allow the liquid to boil or the beef will be tough. Remove the meat to a plate, loosely cover with foil and stand for 5 minutes.

- Meanwhile, place the noodles in a bowl, pour over hot water to cover, then stand for 5 minutes or until the noodles are soft. Drain well, rinse under cold water, then drain again.

- Combine the coriander, mint, chilli, spring onion, carrot, cucumber and drained noodles in a serving bowl. Slice the beef into 2 mm ($1/16$ inch) thick slices, then add to the salad.

- Drizzle the dressing over the salad and toss to combine. Sprinkle with the cashews and serve.

Pasta & noodles

RICE NOODLE, BEEF AND VEGETABLE STIR-FRY

preparation time 15 minutes
cooking time 10 minutes
serves 4

150 g (5½ oz) rump or skirt steak, trimmed and finely sliced
2 teaspoons cornflour (cornstarch)
2 teaspoons oyster sauce
1½ tablespoons soy sauce
1 garlic clove, chopped
2 tablespoons vegetable oil
1 carrot, cut into matchsticks
1 small red capsicum (pepper), sliced

3 baby bok choy (pak choy), sliced into 2.5 cm (1 inch) chunks
500 g (1 lb 2 oz) fresh rice noodles (available from the Asian section in supermarkets or Asian food stores)
100 g (3½ oz/1 cup) bean sprouts, trimmed
chopped red chilli, to serve
coriander (cilantro) leaves, to serve

• Put the sliced steak in a bowl with the cornflour, oyster sauce, 1 teaspoon of the soy sauce and the garlic. Stir to coat well.

• Heat 1 tablespoon of the oil in a wok or large non-stick frying pan over medium–high heat. Stir-fry the meat for 1–2 minutes, or until golden and cooked through. Remove from the wok and set aside.

• Wipe the wok clean, then heat the remaining oil over medium–high heat. Stir-fry the carrot and capsicum for 1–2 minutes, then add the bok choy and cook for another minute, or until it begins to wilt. Add the rice noodles, beef mixture and remaining soy sauce and cook, tossing, for 5–6 minutes, or until the noodles soften and the ingredients are well combined.

• Toss the bean sprouts through, remove from the heat and leave to stand for 1–2 minutes. Serve the noodles sprinkled with chilli and coriander.

FIVE-SPICE LAMB AND SUGARSNAP STIR-FRY

preparation time 10 minutes
cooking time 5 minutes
serves 4

2 garlic cloves, crushed
1 teaspoon five-spice powder
8 lamb fillets, trimmed and thinly
   sliced on the diagonal
200 g (7 oz) dried rice stick noodles
80 ml (2½ fl oz/⅓ cup) hoisin sauce
2 tablespoons soy sauce
1 tablespoon grated fresh ginger

2 tablespoons peanut oil
4 spring onions (scallions), trimmed
   and sliced thickly on the diagonal
300 g (10½ oz) oyster mushrooms,
   quartered
300 g (10½ oz) sugarsnap peas,
   trimmed and strings removed
sliced red chilli, to serve

• Combine the garlic, five-spice powder and a large pinch of sea salt in a bowl.
Add the lamb and toss to coat well. Cover and stand for 10 minutes.

• Place the noodles in a heatproof bowl. Pour over boiling water, cover and
stand for 5–10 minutes or until tender. Drain and set aside to keep warm.

• Combine the hoisin sauce, soy sauce, ginger and 1 tablespoon hot water in
a small bowl.

• Heat 1 teaspoon of the peanut oil in a wok over high heat, add the lamb and
stir-fry for 1 minute, or until just cooked through. Remove to a plate.

• Add the remaining oil to the wok, then add the spring onion, mushrooms and
sugarsnap peas. Stir-fry for 2 minutes, then add the hoisin mixture and lamb.
Cook, stirring, for 1 minute or until heated through. Put the noodles in a serving
bowl, top with the lamb and serve sprinkled with the chilli slices.

Pasta & noodles

PASTA WITH ITALIAN SAUSAGES AND BALSAMIC GLAZE

preparation time 20 minutes
cooking time 25 minutes
serves 2

2 tablespoons olive oil
1 large red onion, cut into wedges
2 garlic cloves, crushed
4 Italian sausages (about 175 g/6 oz), skins removed
3 tablespoons raisins, chopped
2 tablespoon balsamic vinegar
2 teaspoon soft brown sugar

125 ml (4 fl oz/½ cup) chicken or beef stock
125 ml (4 fl oz/½ cup) red wine
3 teaspoons fresh thyme or 1 teaspoon dried, or to taste, plus a few sprigs to serve
200 g (7 oz) fettuccine
shaved parmesan and rocket (arugula) salad, to serve

• Place the oil in a frying pan over medium heat, add the onion and garlic and cook, stirring often, for 5 minutes or until softened. Add the sausages, breaking up the meat with a wooden spoon, and cook, stirring, for 3–4 minutes or until the meat changes colour.

• Add the raisins, vinegar, sugar, stock, red wine and thyme to the pan. Bring the mixture to the boil, then lower the heat and cook for 10–15 minutes, stirring occasionally until the sauce is reduced and thickened.

• Meanwhile, cook the fettuccine in a large saucepan of boiling salted water according to the packet instructions until al dente. Drain well and place in a serving bowl.

• Spoon the sauce over the pasta and serve immediately, garnished with the thyme sprigs and with the shaved parmesan and rocket salad on the side.

RIGATONI WITH SAUSAGE AND TOMATO SUGO

preparation time 15 minutes
cooking time 20 minutes
serves 4

300 g (10½ oz) good-quality Italian
   sausages, skins removed
1 onion, finely chopped
1 carrot, finely chopped
400 g (14 oz) tin chopped tomatoes
2 garlic cloves, crushed

400 g (14 oz) rigatoni
1 handful rocket (arugula), roughly
   chopped
2 tablespoons ligurian or other small
   black olives
shaved parmesan cheese, to serve

• Heat a non-stick frying pan over medium–high heat. Add the sausages and
cook for about 5 minutes, breaking them up with a wooden spoon to crumble
the meat. Add the onion and carrot and sauté for 5 minutes, or until softened.

• Stir in the tomatoes and garlic and reduce the heat to medium. Cook for
a further 8–10 minutes, or until the vegetables are tender and the mixture
has thickened.

• Meanwhile, bring a large saucepan of salted water to the boil. Add the pasta
and cook according to the packet instructions. Drain, reserving about 125 ml
(4 fl oz/½ cup) of the cooking water.

• Stir the drained pasta into the sauce, adding some of the reserved cooking
water to thin the sauce slightly if necessary. Stir the rocket and olives into the
pasta until the leaves just wilt. Season with sea salt and freshly ground black
pepper. Spoon into serving bowls, scatter with parmesan shavings and serve.

Pasta & noodles

BACON, PEA AND WALNUT SPAGHETTI CARBONARA

preparation time 15 minutes
cooking time 20 minutes
serves 4

500 g (1 lb 2 oz) spaghetti
4 slices of bacon (about 400 g/14 oz),
   rind and excess fat removed
1 tablespoon olive oil
3 garlic cloves, finely chopped
155 g (5½ oz/1 cup) frozen peas,
   thawed
4 eggs

75 g (2½ oz/¾ cup) grated
   parmesan cheese
185 ml (6 fl oz/¾ cup) cream
90 g (3¼ oz/¾ cup) toasted
   walnuts, chopped
1 tablespoon chopped flat-leaf
   (Italian) parsley
grated parmesan cheese, to serve

● Bring a large saucepan of salted water to the boil. Add the spaghetti and cook according to the packet instructions.

● Meanwhile, cut the bacon into 5 mm (¼ inch) strips. Heat the oil in a frying pan over medium heat, then add the bacon strips and cook for 5 minutes, or until slightly crisp. Add the garlic and peas. Sauté over low heat for 3 minutes. Remove from the heat and set aside.

● In a small bowl whisk together the eggs, parmesan and cream. Season to taste with sea salt and freshly ground black pepper.

• When the spaghetti is al dente, drain well, then return to the pan and gently toss over low heat for 2 minutes to evaporate any liquid. Toss the bacon and peas through, then add the egg mixture. Stir for 1–2 minutes, taking care not to let the mixture boil or the eggs will scramble. Remove from the heat, cover and leave to stand for 2–3 minutes, or until the sauce thickens.

• Toss the walnuts through the remaining pasta. Serve sprinkled with parsley and extra parmesan.

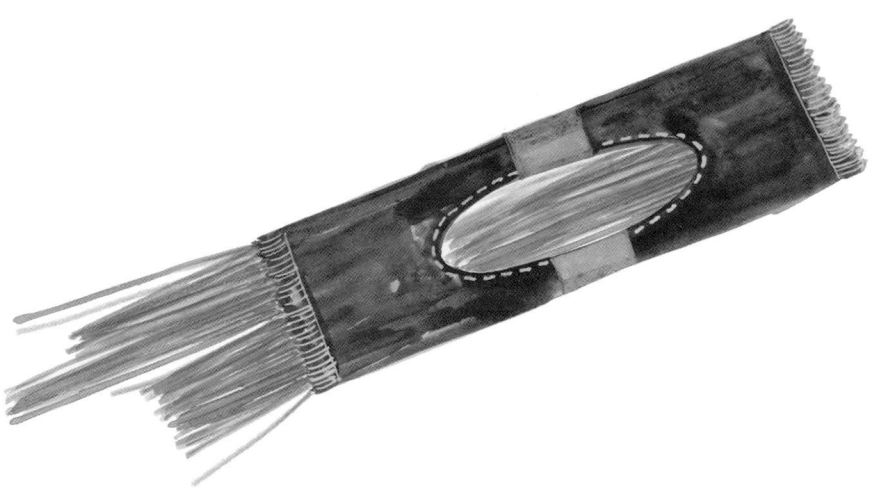

CREAMY BOSCAIOLA

preparation time 15 minutes
cooking time 25 minutes
serves 4

500 g (1 lb 2 oz) spaghetti
1 tablespoon olive oil
6 bacon slices, chopped
200 g (7 oz) button mushrooms,
   sliced

625 ml (21½ fl oz/2½ cups) cream
2 spring onions (scallions), sliced
1 tablespoon chopped flat-leaf
   (Italian) parsley

● Cook the pasta in a large saucepan of rapidly boiling salted water until al dente. Drain, return to the pan and keep warm.

● While the pasta is cooking, heat the oil in a large frying pan, add the bacon and mushroom and cook, stirring, for 5 minutes, or until golden brown.

● Stir in a little of the cream and scrape the wooden spoon on the bottom of the pan to dislodge any bacon that has stuck. Add the remaining cream, bring to the boil and cook over high heat for 15 minutes, or until the sauce is thick enough to coat the back of a spoon. Stir the spring onion through the mixture.

● Pour the sauce over the pasta and toss to combine. Serve sprinkled with the parsley.

RUOTE WITH LEMON, OLIVES AND BACON

preparation time 10 minutes
cooking time 15 minutes
serves 4

500 g (1 lb 2 oz) ruote (wheel-
    shaped pasta)
6 bacon slices
125 g (4½ oz/1 cup) black olives,
    sliced

80 ml (2½ fl oz/⅓ cup) lemon juice
2 teaspoons finely grated lemon zest
80 ml (2½ fl oz/⅓ cup) olive oil
4 tablespoons chopped flat-leaf
    (Italian) parsley

- Cook the pasta in a large saucepan of rapidly boiling salted water until al dente. Drain and return to the pan.

- While the pasta is cooking, discard the bacon rind and cut the bacon into thin strips. Cook in a frying pan until lightly browned.

- In a bowl, combine the olives, lemon juice, lemon zest, olive oil, chopped parsley and the bacon. Gently toss the olive and bacon mixture through the pasta until it is evenly distributed. Season with freshly ground black pepper, to taste.

Pasta & noodles

INDIVIDUAL MACARONI CHEESE AND VEGETABLE BAKES

preparation time 20 minutes
cooking time 45 minutes
serves 4

100 g (3½ oz/⅔ cup) macaroni
1 carrot, finely chopped
1 celery stalk, finely sliced
100 g (3½ oz/¾ cup) frozen baby
    peas
150 g (5½ oz) spicy salami, chopped
3 tablespoons chopped basil

WHITE ONION SAUCE
45 g (1½ oz) butter
1 onion, chopped
2 tablespoons plain (all-purpose) flour
625 ml (21½ fl oz/2½ cups) milk

2 teaspoons dijon mustard
125 g (4½ oz/1 cup) grated cheddar
    cheese

TOPPING
30 g (1 oz) butter
80 g (2¾ oz/1 cup) fresh white
    breadcrumbs
40 g (1½ oz/⅓ cup) grated cheddar
    cheese
35 g (1¼ oz/⅓ cup) grated parmesan
    cheese

• Preheat the oven to 190°C (375°F/Gas 5). Lightly oil four ovenproof dishes, each about 250 ml (9 fl oz/1 cup) capacity, and place on a baking tray.

• Bring a large saucepan of salted water to the boil. Add the macaroni and cook for 7 minutes, then add the carrot and celery and cook for another 2 minutes, or until the vegetables are almost tender. Add the peas and cook for 1 minute, then transfer the macaroni and vegetables to a colander and drain well.

• To make the white onion sauce, melt the butter in a saucepan and sauté the onion over low heat for 4–5 minutes, or until softened but not browned. Add the flour and whisk to a smooth paste. Cook, stirring, for 2–3 minutes, then gradually whisk in the milk until well combined and smooth. Bring the mixture to a simmer while stirring constantly, then continue stirring for 2 minutes, or until the sauce has thickened. Reduce the heat and cook, stirring often, for 5 minutes. Stir in the mustard and cheese and allow to cool slightly.

• Mix the macaroni and vegetables through the white sauce. Stir in the salami and basil and season to taste with sea salt and freshly ground black pepper. Spoon the mixture into the baking dishes.

• To make the topping, melt the butter in a frying pan. Remove from the heat and gently stir in the breadcrumbs. Stir in the grated cheeses, then sprinkle the mixture over the macaroni mixture. Bake for 20 minutes, or until the topping is golden and crisp. Serve hot.

HAM, RICOTTA AND SPINACH CANNELLONI

preparation time 25 minutes
cooking time 35 minutes
serves 6

250 g (9 oz) packet frozen spinach,
    thawed
400 g (14 oz/1⅔ cups) firm fresh
    ricotta cheese
100 g (3½ oz/1 cup) finely grated
    parmesan cheese
200 g (7 oz) leg ham off the bone,
    finely chopped

2 egg yolks
1 garlic clove, crushed
50 g (1¾ oz/⅓ cup) pine nuts,
    chopped
2 tablespoons chopped basil, plus
    extra, to garnish
ground white pepper, to taste
20 instant dried cannelloni shells
    (about 230 g/8 oz)
375 ml (13 fl oz/1½ cups) cream
2½ tablespoons chicken stock
pinch freshly grated nutmeg
halved cherry tomatoes, to garnish

- Preheat the oven to 180°C (350°F/Gas 4).

- Place the spinach in a clean tea towel (dish towel) and squeeze firmly to remove as much water as possible. Finely chop the spinach and put in a bowl with the ricotta, half the parmesan, the ham, egg yolks, garlic, pine nuts and basil. Season with sea salt and ground white pepper and mix together well.

- Spoon the filling into the cannelloni shells, then arrange in a 20 x 32 cm (8 x 13 inch) baking dish (or one of 3.5 litre/122 fl oz/14 cup capacity).

- Mix together the cream, stock and half the remaining parmesan and season to taste. Pour over the cannelloni and sprinkle with the remaining parmesan and nutmeg.

- Cover with foil and bake for 20 minutes, then remove the foil and bake for 15 minutes, or until the top is golden and the sauce is bubbling. Serve hot, garnished with cherry tomatoes and basil.

Pasta & noodles

CHINESE PORK NOODLES

preparation time 20 minutes
cooking time 15 minutes
serves 4

2 tablespoons Chinese yellow bean
   sauce (available from large
   supermarkets and Asian food
   stores)
2 tablespoon hoisin sauce
1 tablespoon soy sauce
1 tablespoon Chinese rice wine
1 tablespoon soft brown sugar
1 teaspoon sesame oil
2 tablespoons peanut oil

1 onion, thinly sliced
2–3 garlic cloves, finely chopped
500 g (1 lb 2 oz) minced (ground)
   pork
400 g (14 oz) fresh egg noodles
1 small cucumber, cut into fine
   matchsticks
2 spring onions (scallions), cut into
   curls or fine matchsticks
chopped roasted peanuts, to serve

• Combine the yellow bean, hoisin and soy sauce in a bowl with the rice wine, sugar, sesame oil and 80 ml (2½ fl oz/⅓ cup) water. Mix well to dissolve the sugar, then set aside.

• Heat a wok over high heat. Add about 1 tablespoon of the peanut oil, then add the onion and garlic and stir-fry for 4–5 minutes, or until golden. Remove to a plate.

• Add the pork to the wok in batches and cook for 2–3 minutes each batch, stirring to break up any lumps, and adding more oil as needed. Remove each batch to a bowl.

• Return the onion mixture and all the pork to the wok. Add the hoisin sauce mixture and stir-fry for 3 minutes, or until the liquid has reduced a little.

• Meanwhile, cook the noodles in a large saucepan of boiling water until just soft, following the packet instructions. Drain well.

• Toss the pork mixture through the noodles. Serve garnished with the cucumber, spring onion and peanuts.

PORK AND EGG PAD THAI

preparation time 30 minutes
cooking time 15 minutes
serves 4

400 g (14 oz) fresh rice noodles
2 tablespoons peanut oil
200 g (7 oz) firm tofu, cut into 2 cm
   (¾ inch) chunks
2 garlic cloves, crushed
1 large pork fillet (about 400 g/
   14 oz), trimmed and very thinly
   sliced
2 eggs
125 g (4½ oz/½ cup) pad Thai paste

1 tablespoon shaved palm sugar
   (jaggery)
2 tablespoons lime juice
80 g (2¾ oz/½ cup) chopped roasted
   peanuts
4 spring onions (scallions), sliced
100 g (3½ oz/1 cup) bean sprouts,
   trimmed
1 large handful coriander (cilantro)
   leaves
lemon wedges, to serve

• Place the noodles in a large heatproof bowl. Pour in enough boiling water
to cover, then leave to soak for 3−4 minutes, or until softened. Loosen with
chopsticks or tongs, then drain well and set aside.

• Meanwhile, heat half the oil in a wok over medium−high heat. Add the tofu
and garlic and stir-fry for 2−3 minutes, or until golden. Remove with a slotted
spoon and drain on paper towels.

• Heat the remaining oil in the wok over high heat. Add the pork in batches
and stir-fry for 4−5 minutes, or until the pork is just cooked, removing each
batch to a bowl.

● Lightly beat the eggs, then add to the wok and cook without stirring for 1–2 minutes, until just set. Break the omelette up a bit, then return the tofu and the pork mixture to the wok. Add the noodles, pad Thai paste, sugar and lime juice and toss well to combine.

● Remove the wok from the heat and toss the peanuts, spring onion, bean sprouts and coriander through the noodle mixture. Divide among warm bowls and serve with lemon wedges.

Pasta & noodles

SWEET AND SOUR PORK NOODLE STIR-FRY

preparation time 20 minutes
cooking time 10 minutes
serves 4

60 ml (2 fl oz/¼ cup) rice vinegar or
    white vinegar
1½ tablespoons soft brown sugar
2½ tablespoons soy sauce
2 teaspoons sesame oil
2 tablespoons vegetable oil
500 g (1 lb 2 oz) pork fillet, trimmed
    and cut into 5 mm (¼ inch) slices
6 spring onions (scallions), cut into
    3 cm (1¼ inch) lengths
3 garlic cloves, finely chopped
1 tablespoon finely chopped fresh
    ginger
1 red capsicum (pepper), cut into
    strips 5 mm (¼ inch) wide
100 g (3½ oz) snow peas
    (mangetout), trimmed and cut
    in half on the diagonal
½ very ripe, small sweet pineapple,
    trimmed, cored and cut into
    1.5 cm (½ inch) chunks

200 g (7 oz) crisp fried noodles
    (available from the Asian section
    of supermarkets)
2 tablespoons chopped coriander
    (cilantro) leaves, plus a few sprigs,
    to garnish

● Put the vinegar, sugar, soy sauce and sesame oil in a bowl and mix well to dissolve the sugar. Set aside.

● Heat 1 ½ tablespoons of the vegetable oil in a large wok until very hot. Add half the pork and cook, tossing the wok constantly, for 1–2 minutes, or until the pork has just changed colour. Remove to a plate using a slotted spoon. Reheat the wok if necessary, cook the remaining pork as before, then remove from the wok and set aside.

● Heat the remaining oil in the wok. Add the spring onion, garlic and ginger and stir-fry over high heat for 2–3 seconds, taking care not to let it burn.

● Add the capsicum, snow peas and pineapple and stir-fry for 2–3 minutes, tossing occasionally, or until the vegetables have heated through and the capsicum has softened.

● Add the soy sauce mixture and pork to the wok, toss to combine and bring just to the boil. Add the noodles and coriander and toss together well. Divide among warm deep bowls, scatter with the coriander sprigs and serve.

Pasta & noodles

CHARGRILLED SQUID AND PASTA SALAD

preparation time 15 minutes
cooking time 15 minutes
serves 2

160 g (6 oz) linguine pasta
2 tomatoes, trimmed and finely diced
1 small head radicchio, shredded
12 flat-leaf (Italian) parsley leaves
12 basil leaves
2 tablespoons Ligurian or other small
    black olives
3 anchovy fillets, finely chopped
1 large garlic clove, crushed

1 tablespoon lemon juice
3 tablespoons olive oil
250 g (9 oz) cleaned squid tubes and
    tentacles, tubes cut open
    and inside surface scored finely
    with a small, sharp knife
lemon wedges, to serve

● Cook the linguine in a saucepan of boiling, salted water for 12 minutes or according to the packet instructions until al dente. Drain, then cool under cold water and drain again.

● Combine the tomato, radicchio, parsley, basil and olives in a bowl, then add the linguine and toss to combine. Lightly whisk together the anchovy, garlic, lemon juice and olive oil. Drizzle over the pasta salad.

● Heat a chargrill pan over high heat or a barbecue to high. Cook the squid tubes and tentacles for 3 minutes, turning once, or until lightly charred and cooked through. Add to the salad, toss well to combine and serve immediately with lemon wedges.

FARFALLE WITH TUNA, CAPERS AND LEMON CREAM SAUCE

preparation time 10 minutes
cooking time 15 minutes
serves 4

650 g (1 lb 7 oz) tuna fillet, trimmed
250 g (9 oz) farfalle pasta
250 ml (9 fl oz/1 cup) cream
4 handfuls baby rocket (arugula)

2½ tablespoons small capers, drained
2 teaspoons finely grated lemon rind
2½ tablespoons lemon juice
pinch dried chilli flakes (optional)

● Using a large, sharp knife, cut the tuna into 1 cm (½ inch) pieces. Set aside.

● Cook the pasta in boiling, salted water for 13 minutes or according to the packet instructions until al dente. Drain well.

● Combine the cream, rocket and capers in a small saucepan or frying pan over medium–low heat, cover and bring to a gentle boil. Add the lemon rind and stir to combine well, then cook for 1 minute, or until the rocket is just wilted. Add the tuna, lemon juice and pasta to the pan, toss to combine well and heat for 30–40 seconds to warm the tuna through. Season with sea salt, freshly ground black pepper and chilli flakes, if using. Serve immediately.

Pasta & noodles

ORECCHIETTE WITH TUNA, LEMON AND CAPER SAUCE

preparation time 10 minutes
cooking time 20 minutes
serves 4

500 g (1 lb 2 oz) orecchiette
30 g (1 oz) butter
1 garlic clove, crushed
1 onion, finely chopped
425 g (15 oz) tinned tuna in brine,
    drained
2 tablespoons lemon juice

250 ml (9 fl oz/1 cup) cream
2 tablespoons chopped flat-leaf
    (Italian) parsley
1 tablespoon capers, drained
¼ teaspoon cayenne pepper
    (optional)
caperberries, to garnish (optional)

● Cook the orecchiette in a large saucepan of rapidly boiling salted water until al dente. Drain and return to the pan.

● Heat the butter in a saucepan and cook the garlic and onion for 1–2 minutes. Add the tuna, lemon juice, cream, half the parsley and the capers. Season with black pepper and cayenne, if using. Simmer over low heat for 5 minutes.

● Add the tuna sauce to the pasta and toss until thoroughly combined. Serve the pasta sprinkled with the remaining parsley, and garnish with caperberries, if desired.

SPAGHETTI PUTTANESCA

preparation time 20 minutes
cooking time 25 minutes
serves 4–6

2 tablespoons olive oil
1 onion, finely chopped
2–3 garlic cloves, finely chopped
1 small carrot, finely diced
1 celery stalk, finely diced
800 g (1 lb 12 oz) tinned peeled,
  chopped tomatoes or 1 kg
  (2 lb 4 oz) ripe tomatoes, peeled
  and chopped

1 tablespoon tomato paste
  (concentrated purée)
3 tablespoons shredded basil
500 g (1 lb 2 oz) penne
freshly grated parmesan cheese,
  to serve (optional)

● Heat the olive oil in a large frying pan. Add the onion and garlic and cook
for 2 minutes, or until golden. Add the carrot and celery and cook for another
2 minutes.

● Add the chopped tomato and the tomato paste. Simmer for 20 minutes,
or until the sauce thickens, stirring occasionally. Stir in the shredded basil
and season to taste.

● While the sauce is cooking, cook the pasta in a large saucepan of rapidly
boiling salted water until al dente. Drain well and return to the pan.

● Add the sauce to the pasta and mix well. Serve with grated parmesan
cheese, if desired.

Pasta & noodles

Meat & fish dishes

The aroma of grills, roasts, barbecued dishes and curries is simply irresistible, and the flavours are hard to beat.

CUMIN-DUSTED CHICKEN WITH CORN, BEAN AND AVOCADO SALAD

preparation time 20 minutes
cooking time 20 minutes
serves 4

55 g (2 oz/½ cup) besan (chickpea flour), available from Indian grocers and health food stores
1 teaspoon ground cumin
2 eggs
750 g (1 lb 10 oz/about 12) chicken tenderloins, trimmed of sinew
olive oil, for pan-frying

CORN, BEAN AND AVOCADO SALAD
2 corn cobs, husks and silk removed
1 avocado, cut into thin wedges
2 tomatoes, cut into 1 cm (½ inch) chunks
400 g (14 oz) tin red kidney beans, rinsed and drained
60 ml (2 fl oz/¼ cup) extra virgin olive oil
2 tablespoons lemon juice
½ teaspoon Tabasco sauce, or to taste
1 small handful coriander (cilantro) leaves, roughly chopped

● To make the salad, cook the corn cobs in a saucepan of boiling salted water for 8–10 minutes, or until the kernels are tender. Drain well and cool. Using a large sharp knife, remove the kernels from the cobs and place in a bowl with the avocado, tomato and beans. Whisk together the olive oil, lemon juice and Tabasco sauce, season with sea salt and freshly ground black pepper, then pour over the salad. Add the coriander and toss gently to combine. Set aside.

● Mix together the besan and cumin in a bowl and season with salt and pepper. Break the eggs into a bowl and lightly beat. Dust the chicken with the besan mixture, shaking off the excess, then dip into the beaten egg, draining off the excess. Dip in the besan mixture again to coat well.

● Heat about 1 cm (½ inch) olive oil in a large, deep frying pan over medium–high heat. Cook the chicken in two batches, frying for 2 minutes on each side, or until golden and cooked through. Drain well on paper towels.

● Serve the chicken immediately with the salad.

CHINESE POACHED CHICKEN WITH BOK CHOY

preparation time 10 minutes
cooking time 20 minutes
serves 2

165 ml (5½ fl oz) soy sauce
165 ml (5½ fl oz) Chinese rice wine
90 g (3 oz) grated palm
   sugar (jaggery)
1 star anise
2.5 cm (1 inch) strip orange zest,
   all white pith removed
3 cm (1 inch) piece ginger,
   thinly sliced
2 garlic cloves, thinly sliced

2 large chicken breast fillets,
   cut in half widthways
3 teaspoons peanut oil
1 large red capsicum (pepper),
   halved lengthways, seeded and
   cut into 1 cm (½ inch) strips
250 g (8 oz, about 4) baby bok choy
   (pak choy), trimmed and cut in half
   lengthways
steamed rice, to serve

- Combine the soy sauce, rice wine, sugar, star anise, orange zest, ginger, half the garlic and 150 ml (5 fl oz) water in a small saucepan. Cover and slowly bring to the boil over medium–low heat. Reduce the heat to low and gently boil for 5 minutes.

- Add the chicken, cover and cook over very low heat for 5 minutes; the liquid should be barely boiling. Don't let the liquid come to a full boil or the chicken will be tough. Without removing the lid, remove the pan from the heat and stand for 20 minutes to allow the chicken to cook through and the flavours to develop.

- Heat the oil in a wok over high heat, then add the capsicum and cook, tossing the wok, for 2 minutes or until slightly charred and softened. Add the bok choy and remaining garlic and cook, tossing often, for 1–2 minutes or until the bok choy begins to soften. Add 3 tablespoons of the chicken cooking liquid to the wok and cook for 1 minute or until the liquid has reduced slightly and the vegetables are tender.

- Serve the chicken with the vegetables and steamed rice.

JERK CHICKEN

preparation time 20 minutes plus 8 hours marinating
cooking time 35 minutes
serves 4

1.2 kg (2 lb 10 oz) chicken, cut into
    8 pieces
1 small sweet potato, about 300 g
    (10½ oz), peeled and cut into
    2 cm (¾ inch) chunks
½ ripe pineapple, cut into 4 cm
    (1½ inch) chunks
1 tablespoon olive oil
1½ tablespoons lime juice
1 small handful coriander (cilantro)
    leaves
100 g (3½ oz) mixed salad leaves

THYME AND CHILLI MARINADE
1 onion, roughly chopped
1–2 long red chillies, roughly chopped
80 ml (2½ fl oz/⅓ cup) white wine
    vinegar
80 ml (2½ fl oz/⅓ cup) dark soy sauce
1 tablespoon finely chopped fresh
    ginger
10 g (¼ oz/½ bunch) thyme,
    leaves picked
1 teaspoon ground allspice

• Combine all the thyme and chilli marinade ingredients in a food processor
and blend until a paste forms. Transfer to a large bowl, add all the chicken
pieces and toss to coat, rubbing the marinade in well. Cover and marinate in
the refrigerator for 8 hours, or overnight.

• Preheat the oven to 180°C (350°F/Gas 4).

• In a large bowl, toss the sweet potato and pineapple with the olive oil and
lime juice, then spread in a roasting tin.

● Place the undrained chicken pieces in another roasting tin, then put both tins in the oven and roast for 35 minutes, or until the chicken is cooked through and the sweet potato is tender.

● Toss the pineapple and sweet potato in a bowl with the coriander and salad leaves. Divide among serving plates or shallow bowls. Top with the chicken pieces, drizzle with the juices from the roasting tin and serve.

MALAY-STYLE CHICKEN CURRY

preparation time 30 minutes
cooking time 30 minutes
serves 2

2 tablespoons vegetable oil
2 teaspoons Malay curry powder,
   or to taste
500 g (1 lb 2 oz) boneless, skinless
   chicken thighs, trimmed and cut
   into 4 cm (1½ inch) pieces
1 small cinnamon stick
½ star anise
1 lemongrass stem, trimmed
   and bruised
165 ml (5½ fl oz) tin coconut milk
400 g (14 oz) tin diced tomatoes
150 g (5¼ oz) sweet potato, peeled
   and cut into 2 cm (¾ inch) pieces
50 g (1¾ oz) green beans, trimmed
2 teaspoons grated palm sugar
   (jaggery), or soft brown sugar
2 teaspoons fish sauce
2 teaspoons lime juice
200 g (7 oz) long-grain rice
lime cheek, to serve

SPICE PASTE
1 small onion, roughly chopped
2 cm (¾ inch) piece ginger,
   peeled and chopped
3 garlic cloves

- To make the spice paste, blend all the ingredients in a small food processor until a paste-like consistency.

- Heat the oil in a saucepan over medium−low heat. Stir in the spice paste and cook until softened and translucent. Add the curry powder, chicken, cinnamon, star anise and lemongrass. Stir to coat the chicken, then cook for 1−2 minutes, or until aromatic.

- Increase the heat to medium−high, then add the coconut milk, tomato and sweet potato. Season to taste with sea salt, bring to the boil, then reduce the heat to low and cook, covered, for 20 minutes, stirring occasionally.

- Add the beans and cook for 5 minutes, or until the vegetables are cooked and the chicken is tender. Stir in the sugar, fish sauce and lime juice, adding extra sugar, fish sauce or lime juice to taste, if necessary.

- Meanwhile, combine the rice and 500 ml (17 fl oz/2 cups) water in a small saucepan over a high heat. Bring to the boil and cover with a lid. Reduce the heat to medium−low and gently cook for 12−15 minutes or until all the water is absorbed.

- Serve the chicken with the lime cheek and rice on the side.

Meat & fish dishes

STEAMED CANTONESE CHICKEN WITH GINGER AND SNOW PEAS

preparation time 15 minutes plus 30 minutes marinating
cooking time 20 minutes
serves 4

4 small boneless, skinless chicken
   breasts (about 600 g/1 lb 5 oz
   in total), cut on the diagonal into
   slices 2 cm (¾ inch) thick
1½ teaspoons cornflour (cornstarch)
1 garlic clove, chopped
2 cm (¾ inch) knob of fresh ginger,
   peeled and cut into thin
   matchsticks
pinch Chinese five-spice, or to taste
1 tablespoon oyster sauce
2 teaspoons soy sauce, plus extra,
   to serve

1 tablespoon hoisin sauce, plus extra,
   to serve
6 dried shiitake mushrooms
2 spring onions (scallions), cut into
   2 cm (¾ inch) lengths
100 g (3½ oz) snow peas
   (mangetout), thinly sliced
   lengthways
4 baby bok choy (pak choy), trimmed,
   leaves halved lengthways
400 g (14 oz) fresh rice noodles

● Put the chicken in a bowl with the cornflour, garlic, ginger, five-spice, oyster sauce, soy sauce and hoisin sauce. Toss well to coat the chicken, then cover and marinate in the refrigerator or at cool room temperature for 30 minutes.

● Meanwhile, soak the mushrooms in boiling water for 20 minutes, or until they are softened. Drain well, then cut off and discard the stems. Thinly slice the mushrooms and set aside.

● Place the chicken mixture in a dish that holds all the chicken in a single layer and will fit inside a large steamer. Place the mushrooms on top of the chicken. Bring some water to the boil in the base of the steamer, then place the chicken dish in and cover the steamer (the dish the chicken is sitting in shouldn't touch the water in the steamer). Cook for 10 minutes, then place the spring onion, snow peas and bok choy over the chicken. Cover and steam for 5 minutes, or until the vegetables are tender and the chicken is cooked through.

● Meanwhile, place the noodles in a heatproof bowl, pour in enough boiling water to cover and leave to soak for 2–3 minutes, or until softened. Loosen the noodles with chopsticks or tongs, then drain well.

● Divide the noodles among warm bowls and top with the vegetables and chicken. Serve with extra soy sauce and hoisin sauce for drizzling over.

ROAST CHICKEN TENDERLOINS IN PANCETTA WITH CAULIFLOWER PURÉE

preparation time 20 minutes
cooking time 20 minutes
serves 4

12 chicken tenderloins, about 750 g
(1 lb 10 oz) in total, or 4 boneless,
skinless chicken breasts, sliced on
the diagonal into thirds
12 large basil leaves
12 thin slices of mild pancetta, about
200 g (7 oz) in total
olive oil, for brushing
1 large cauliflower, about 700 g
(1 lb 9 oz) in total, cut into florets

25 g (1 oz/¼ cup) grated parmesan
60 g (2¼ oz/¼ cup) crème fraiche
or sour cream
½ teaspoon thyme or finely snipped
chives
¼ teaspoon grated orange rind
(optional)
lemon wedges, to serve
green leaf salad, to serve

- Preheat the oven to 190°C (375°F/Gas 5).

- Season the chicken with sea salt and freshly ground black pepper. Lay a basil leaf on top of each piece, then wrap a pancetta slice around each one, tucking the edges underneath the chicken to enclose it. Brush the pancetta lightly with oil, then transfer to a lightly oiled roasting tin and roast for 17–18 minutes, or until the pancetta is crisp and the chicken is cooked through.

- Meanwhile, working in batches if necessary, place the cauliflower florets in a steamer basket set over a large saucepan of boiling water. Cover and cook for 4 minutes, or until tender.

- Transfer the cauliflower to a food processor with the parmesan, crème fraiche, thyme and orange rind, if using. Blend until smooth, then season to taste.

- Arrange three chicken tenderloins on each serving plate and spoon the cauliflower purée alongside. Serve with lemon wedges and a green leaf salad.

TANDOORI ROAST CHICKEN

preparation time 20 minutes plus 4 hours marinating
cooking time 40 minutes
serves 4

1.4 kg (3 lb 2 oz) chicken, cut into
    8 pieces
2 Lebanese (short) cucumbers,
    cut lengthways and seeded
150 g (5½ oz) Greek-style yoghurt
1 small red onion, thinly sliced
2 vine-ripened tomatoes, chopped
1 small handful coriander (cilantro)
    leaves
1 tablespoon lemon juice
naan bread, to serve
lemon wedges, to serve

TANDOORI MARINADE
1 small onion, grated
1 teaspoon ground coriander
1 teaspoon finely grated fresh ginger
1 teaspoon finely grated lemon rind
2 teaspoons lemon juice
2 tablespoons tandoori paste
½ teaspoon sea salt
80 g (2¾ oz/⅓ cup) Greek-style
    yoghurt

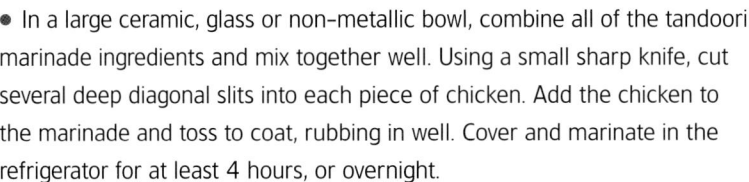

- In a large ceramic, glass or non-metallic bowl, combine all of the tandoori marinade ingredients and mix together well. Using a small sharp knife, cut several deep diagonal slits into each piece of chicken. Add the chicken to the marinade and toss to coat, rubbing in well. Cover and marinate in the refrigerator for at least 4 hours, or overnight.

- Preheat the oven to 220°C (425°C/Gas 7). Drain the chicken well and discard the marinade. Arrange the chicken in a single layer on a greased wire rack set over a baking tray. Transfer to the oven and roast for 40 minutes, or until the chicken is cooked through.

- Meanwhile, roughly grate one of the cucumbers, then use your hands to squeeze out the excess liquid. Combine the cucumber in a small bowl with the yoghurt. Mix well and set aside.

● Chop the remaining cucumber and combine in another bowl with the onion, tomato, coriander and lemon juice.

● Serve the tandoori chicken with the tomato salad, cucumber–yoghurt sauce, naan bread and lemon wedges.

SINGAPORE CHICKEN CURRY WITH PINEAPPLE AND CUCUMBER SALSA

preparation time 15 minutes
cooking time 40 minutes
serves 4–6

1½ tablespoons peanut oil
1 onion, thinly sliced
800 g (1 lb 12 oz) boneless, skinless
  chicken thighs, trimmed and cut
  into 4 cm (1½ inch) chunks
185 g (6½ oz) jar Malaysian curry
  paste
2 potatoes, peeled and cut into 2 cm
  (¾ inch) chunks
400 ml (14 fl oz) tin coconut milk
1 red capsicum (pepper), thinly sliced
steamed rice, to serve
coriander (cilantro) leaves, to serve

PINEAPPLE AND CUCUMBER
  SALSA
1 Lebanese (short) cucumber, seeded
  and chopped
125 g (4½ oz/1 cup) fresh pineapple
  chunks
1 long red chilli, seeded and cut into
  long strips
2 tablespoons rice vinegar
1 tablespoon shaved palm sugar
  (jaggery)
2 teaspoons fish sauce
1 teaspoon lemon juice

● Heat half the oil in a wok or large frying pan over high heat. Add the onion
and sauté for 2 minutes, or until just softened. Remove the onion to a plate.

● Heat the remaining oil in the wok. Add the chicken in batches and stir-fry for
5 minutes, or until golden. Remove to a plate.

● Return the onion to the wok, add the curry paste and cook, stirring, for
1 minute, or until aromatic. Add the potatoes, chicken, coconut milk and
125 ml (4 fl oz/½ cup) water and bring to the boil. Reduce the heat to low,
cover and simmer for 15 minutes, until the potatoes and chicken are tender.
Add the capsicum and cook for a further 2 minutes, or until just softened.

● Meanwhile, put all the pineapple and cucumber salsa ingredients in a large
ceramic or glass bowl with a pinch of salt. Stir to combine, then cover and set
aside for 10 minutes to allow the flavours to develop.

● Serve the chicken curry with the pineapple and cucumber salsa and steamed
rice, garnished with coriander leaves.

PARMESAN-CRUMBED VEAL WITH MIXED VEGETABLE MASH

preparation time 25 minutes
cooking time 20 minutes
serves 6

160 g (5¾ oz/2 cups) fresh white
　breadcrumbs
50 g (1¾ oz/½ cup) finely grated
　parmesan cheese
75 g (2½ oz/½ cup) plain
　(all-purpose) flour
2 eggs
1 garlic clove, crushed
6 thin slices of veal (about 350 g/
　12 oz in total), pounded very thinly
　using a meat mallet
20 g (¾ oz) butter
2 tablespoons olive oil
lemon wedges, to serve

MIXED VEGETABLE MASH
500 g (1 lb 2 oz) butternut pumpkin
　(winter squash), peeled and
　chopped
2 potatoes, peeled and chopped
155 g (5½ oz/1 cup) frozen peas
20 g (¾ oz) butter
60 ml (2 fl oz/¼ cup) warm milk

● To make the mixed vegetable mash, bring a saucepan of lightly salted water to the boil, add the pumpkin and potato and cook for 10–15 minutes, or until nearly tender. Add the peas and cook for 1 minute. Drain well, then return the vegetables to the saucepan. Add the butter and milk, season to taste with sea salt and freshly ground black pepper and mash lightly. Cover and keep warm.

● In a large bowl, mix together the breadcrumbs and parmesan. Put the flour in a large bowl and season well. Break the eggs into another bowl and whisk with the garlic.

- Dip each slice of veal into the flour, shaking off the excess. Working with one piece of veal at a time, dip each slice into the egg mixture, allowing the excess to drain off, then dip into the breadcrumb mixture, pressing the crumbs firmly on both sides to coat well.

- Heat half the butter and half the oil in a large, heavy-based frying pan over medium heat. Lay half the veal slices in the pan and cook for 1–1 ½ minutes on each side, or until the crumbs are golden and the veal is cooked through. Keep warm and repeat with the remaining oil, butter and veal.

- Serve immediately, with the mash and lemon wedges.

BAKED ARTICHOKE AND LEMON VEAL CHOPS

preparation time 20 minutes
cooking time 30 minutes
serves 4

60 ml (2 fl oz/¼ cup) olive oil
4 veal chops, about 800 g
   (1 lb 12 oz) in total
1 onion, finely diced
2 garlic cloves, crushed
1 celery stalk, finely diced
2 rindless bacon slices, about 115 g
   (4 oz) in total, finely chopped
2 tablespoons plain (all-purpose) flour
500 ml (17 fl oz/2 cups) chicken stock
280 g (10 oz) jar of artichoke hearts,
   drained and cut in half lengthways

2 teaspoons finely grated lemon rind
2½ tablespoons lemon juice
steamed green beans, to serve
1 small handful flat-leaf (Italian)
   parsley, chopped (optional)

SOFT POLENTA
250 ml (9 fl oz/1 cup) milk
250 ml (9 fl oz/1 cup) chicken stock
150 g (5½ oz/1 cup) instant polenta
50 g (1¾ oz/½ cup) grated parmesan
60 ml (2 fl oz/¼ cup) cream

● Preheat the oven to 180°C (350°F/Gas 4).

● Heat 2 tablespoons of the olive oil in a large frying pan over medium heat. Cook the veal chops in batches for 1 minute on each side, or until golden. Transfer to a baking dish.

● Reduce the heat to medium–low and heat the remaining olive oil in the frying pan. Add the onion and garlic and sauté for 1 minuter until the onion starts to soften. Add the celery and bacon and cook for a further 2 minutes, or until the bacon is golden.

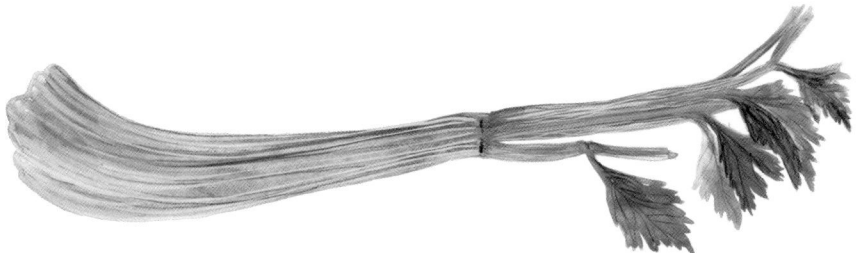

- Sprinkle the flour over and cook, stirring constantly, for 30 seconds, or until combined. Gradually pour in the stock, stirring until well combined and smooth. Bring to a simmer, stirring constantly to prevent lumps forming, then cook for 2–3 minutes, or until the sauce has thickened. Stir in the artichokes, lemon rind and lemon juice.

- Spoon the sauce over the veal chops and bake for 10 minutes, or until the veal is tender.

- Meanwhile, for the soft polenta, combine the milk and stock in a heavy-based saucepan. Bring to the boil over medium heat, then whisk in the polenta. Simmer, stirring constantly with a wooden spoon, for 2–3 minutes, or until the polenta thickens. Stir the parmesan and cream through and season to taste with sea salt and freshly ground black pepper.

- Serve the chops with the soft polenta and steamed beans, sprinkled with the parsley if desired.

COCONUT BEEF WITH PINEAPPLE AND SWEET POTATO SALAD

preparation time 30 minutes plus at least 3 hours marinating
cooking time 25 minutes
serves 4

125 ml (4 fl oz/½ cup) coconut cream
¾ teaspoon ground turmeric
1 garlic clove, crushed
2 teaspoons grated ginger
1 teaspoon light soy sauce
4 x 130 g (4¾ oz) beef minute steaks

PINEAPPLE AND SWEET POTATO SALAD

200 g (7 oz) pineapple (about ¼ small pineapple), peeled, cored and sliced
vegetable oil, for brushing
350 g (12 oz) sweet potato, thinly sliced
2 tablespoons roasted peanuts, roughly chopped
1 red bird's eye chilli, seeded and chopped
1 large handful coriander (cilantro) leaves
150 g (5½ oz/1⅔ cups) bean sprouts
2 tablespoons lime juice
1½ tablespoons soft brown sugar
1 tablespoon fish sauce

● In a large bowl, combine the coconut cream, turmeric, garlic, ginger, and soy sauce. Add the beef and toss to coat. Cover and refrigerate for at least 3 hours.

● About 15 minutes before you are ready to cook the beef, make the pineapple and sweet potato salad. Heat a chargrill pan over medium heat until it reaches smoking point. Lightly brush the pineapple slices with oil and chargrill each side for 2–3 minutes or until golden. Set aside in a large bowl. Repeat the process with the sweet potato, cooking it for 3–4 minutes each side, or until tender and lightly charred. Toss together with the peanuts, chilli, coriander leaves and bean sprouts. Place the lime juice, brown sugar and fish sauce in a small bowl and stir until the sugar dissolves, then toss through the salad.

● To cook the steaks, chargrill for 1–2 minutes each side until browned and just cooked through; take care not to overcook the meat or it will be tough. Slice the meat into 2 cm (¾ inch) slices on the diagonal.

● To serve, divide the salad among serving plates, top with a few slices of beef and serve immediately.

Meat & fish dishes

MEXICAN MEATBALL SOUP

preparation time 20 minutes plus 30 minutes chilling
cooking time 40 minutes
serves 6

2 tablespoons olive oil
1 onion, finely chopped
1 garlic clove, chopped
1 teaspoon ground cumin
250 ml (9 fl oz/1 cup) ready-made
  Mexican salsa
400 g (14 oz) tin chopped tomatoes
1 litre (35 fl oz/4 cups) beef stock
400 g (14 oz) tin red kidney beans,
  rinsed and drained
1 small handful coriander (cilantro)
  leaves, chopped
60 g (2¼ oz/½ cup) grated cheddar
  cheese
sour cream, to serve
corn chips, to serve (optional)

MEATBALLS
500 g (1 lb 2 oz) minced (ground)
  beef
60 g (2¼ oz/½ cup) grated cheddar
  cheese

40 g (1½ oz/½ cup) fresh
  breadcrumbs
2 egg yolks
1 garlic clove, chopped
1 small handful coriander (cilantro)
  leaves, chopped
2 tablespoons lime juice
½ teaspoon ground chilli, or to taste
1 teaspoon dried oregano
1 teaspoon ground cumin

• For the meatballs, combine all the ingredients in a bowl and season well with sea salt and freshly ground black pepper. Using wet hands, roll heaped teaspoons of the mixture into balls. Place on a tray, cover with plastic wrap and refrigerate for 30 minutes, or until required.

• Heat 1½ tablespoons of the olive oil in a large non-stick saucepan over medium–high heat. Cook the meatballs in batches, turning regularly, for 2–3 minutes, or until golden. Set aside.

• Heat the remaining oil in the pan and sauté the onion for 4–5 minutes, or until softened. Add the garlic and cumin and cook for another minute. Stir in the salsa, tomatoes, stock and kidney beans. Bring to the boil, reduce the heat to medium and simmer for 15 minutes. Add the meatballs and coriander and simmer for 5 minutes, or until the meatballs are heated through.

• Divide the soup and meatballs among warm bowls. Scatter with the cheese, add a dollop of sour cream and serve with corn chips, if desired.

JAPANESE BEEF AND POTATO STEW

preparation time 10 minutes
cooking time 50 minutes
serves 4–6

1 tablespoon vegetable oil
1 kg (2 lb 4 oz) beef rump, cut into
   3 cm (1¼ inch) chunks
1 onion, thinly sliced
2 carrots, cut into 1 cm (½ inch)
   rounds
2 red potatoes, peeled and cut into
   3 cm (1¼ inch) chunks
½ teaspoon dashi powder, mixed with
   250 ml (9 fl oz/1 cup) water

125 ml (4 fl oz/½ cup) mirin
2 tablespoons caster (superfine) sugar
60 ml (2 fl oz/¼ cup) Japanese soy
   sauce
200 g (7 oz) fresh udon noodles
2 spring onions (scallions), shredded
   on the diagonal

● Heat the oil in a large heavy-based casserole dish over medium–high heat.
Add the beef in batches and cook, turning often, until browned all over.

● Add the onion, carrot, potato, dashi stock, mirin, sugar and 250 ml (9 fl oz/
1 cup) water. Bring to the boil, reduce the heat to medium–low and simmer for
35 minutes, or until the beef and potatoes are tender.

● Add the soy sauce and noodles, then cover and simmer for 3 minutes, or
until the noodles are heated through.

● Divide among warm bowls and serve sprinkled with the spring onion.

MINUTE STEAK WITH BRANDY CREAM

preparation time 5 minutes
cooking time 10 minutes
serves 2

minute steak (about 250 g/9 oz)
2 tablespoons butter
1 large garlic clove, crushed
3 tablespoons brandy
2 teaspoons dijon mustard
90 ml (3 fl oz) cream

3 teaspoons lemon juice
½ baby cos (romaine) lettuce,
    cut in wedges
lemon wedges and sliced baguette,
    to serve

• Beat the steak thinly if it is not already thin and even, and slice into serving pieces. Season well on both sides with sea salt and freshly ground black pepper. Melt the butter in a heavy-based frying pan over medium–high heat. Cook the steak for 1 minute on each side or until browned. Remove from pan; set aside.

• Reduce the heat to medium–low. Add the garlic to the pan and cook for 30 seconds. Add the brandy and bring to the boil. Cook, stirring, for 1 minute or until half the liquid has evaporated. Reduce the heat to low. Add the mustard and cream and cook, stirring, for 1–2 minutes or until the sauce has thickened slightly. Remove from the heat and season to taste.

• Pour the lemon juice over the lettuce wedges and place on two serving plates. Place the steaks alongside the lettuce and top with the brandy sauce. Serve immediately with the lemon wedges and bread on the side.

Meat & fish dishes

MARINATED STEAK STIR-FRY

preparation time 20 minutes plus 30 minutes marinating
cooking time 15 minutes
serves 4

400 g (14 oz) beef eye fillet or
    minute steak, thinly sliced
60 ml (2 fl oz/¼ cup) peanut oil
1 large red onion, thinly sliced
1 teaspoon finely grated fresh ginger
175 g (6 oz/1 bunch) broccolini,
    trimmed and thinly sliced on
    the diagonal
1 yellow capsicum (pepper),
    thinly sliced
1 tablespoon fish sauce
1 long red chilli, cut into long,
    thin strips
steamed jasmine rice, to serve
lime wedges, to serve

SOY AND LIME MARINADE
1½ tablespoons chopped coriander
    (cilantro) stems and roots
1 small garlic clove, crushed
1 tablespoon shaved palm sugar
    (jaggery)
1 tablespoon oyster sauce
1 tablespoon light soy sauce
1 tablespoon lime juice

Quick & Easy

• Place the soy and lime marinade ingredients in a large bowl and mix until the sugar has dissolved. Add the beef slices and toss to coat well. Cover and marinate in the refrigerator for 3 hours.

• Drain the beef well, reserving the marinade. Place a wok over high heat. Add half the peanut oil and cook the beef in batches for 2 minutes, or until browned, tossing regularly. Remove from the wok and set aside.

• Heat the remaining oil in the wok. Add the onion, ginger, broccolini and capsicum and stir-fry for 2–3 minutes, until the vegetables are just tender. Add the beef slices, reserved marinade and fish sauce and toss until the beef is heated through.

• Divide among serving bowls and garnish with the chilli strips. Serve with steamed jasmine rice and lime wedges.

Meat & fish dishes

LAMB AND PINE NUT RISSOLES

preparation time 20 minutes
cooking time 35 minutes
serves 4

2 tablespoons olive oil, plus extra,
 for drizzling
1 small onion, finely diced
1−2 garlic cloves, crushed
1 teaspoon ground coriander
½ teaspoon ground allspice
½ teaspoon sweet paprika
½ teaspoon ground turmeric
500 g (1 lb 2 oz) minced (ground)
 lamb

1 egg, lightly beaten
40 g (1½ oz/¼ cup) pine nuts, toasted
1 very small handful mint leaves,
 chopped
1 tablespoon tomato paste
 (concentrated purée)
150 g (5½ oz) mixed salad leaves
¼ red onion, thinly sliced
250 g (9 oz/1 cup) baba ghanoush

● Preheat the oven to 180°C (350°F/Gas 4). Heat half the olive oil in a large
frying pan over low heat. Add the onion and garlic and sauté for 5 minutes, or
until softened. Add the ground spices and cook, stirring, for 2 minutes, or until
fragrant. Set aside to cool.

● Place the lamb in a bowl with the egg, pine nuts, mint and tomato paste.
Season and mix until well combined. Add the cooled onion mixture. Mix well,
then shape into eight rissoles.

● Heat the remaining oil in a large frying pan over medium heat. Add the
rissoles, in batches if necessary, and cook for 4 minutes on each side, or
until browned. Transfer the rissoles to a large baking dish and bake for
8−10 minutes, or until cooked through.

● Place the salad leaves in a bowl with the red onion. Drizzle with extra olive
oil and toss to combine. Serve the rissoles with the salad and baba ghanoush.

SHISH KEBABS WITH CAPSICUM AND HERBS

preparation time 20 minutes plus at least 4 hours marinating
cooking time 5 minutes
serves 4

1 kg (2 lb 4 oz) boneless leg of lamb
1 red capsicum (pepper)
1 green capsicum (pepper)
3 red onions

MARINADE
1 onion, thinly sliced
2 garlic cloves, crushed
60 ml (2 fl oz/¼ cup) lemon juice

80 ml (2½ fl oz/⅓ cup) olive oil
1 tablespoon chopped thyme
1 tablespoon paprika
½ teaspoon chilli flakes
2 teaspoons ground cumin
15 g (½ oz) chopped flat-leaf (Italian) parsley
20 g (¾ oz) chopped mint

● If using wooden skewers, soak them for about 30 minutes to prevent them from burning during cooking.

● Trim the sinew and most of the fat from the lamb and cut the meat into 3 cm (1¼ inch) cubes. Combine the marinate ingredients in a large bowl. Season well, add the lamb and mix well. Cover and refrigerate for 4–6 hours, or overnight.

● Remove the seeds and membrane from the capsicums and cut the flesh into 3 cm (1¼ inch) squares. Cut each red onion into six wedges. Remove the lamb from the marinade and reserve the liquid. Thread the meat onto the skewers, alternating with onion and capsicum pieces.

● Grill (broil) the lamb skewers for 5–6 minutes, brushing frequently with the marinade for the first couple of minutes. Serve immediately. These are delicious served with bread or pilaff.

Meat & fish dishes

155

MINTED RACKS OF LAMB

preparation time 15 minutes
cooking time 45 minutes
serves 4

4 x 4-cutlet racks of lamb
300 g (10½ oz/1 cup) mint jelly
2 tablespoons white wine
3 tablespoons finely chopped chives

• Preheat the oven to 200°C (400°F/Gas 6). Trim any excess fat from the lamb, leaving a thin layer of fat, and clean any meat or sinew from the ends of the bones using a small sharp knife. Cover the bones with foil. Place on a rack in a baking dish.

• Mix the mint jelly and white wine together in a saucepan over high heat. Bring to the boil and boil for 4 minutes, or until the mixture is reduced and thickened. Cool slightly, add the chives, then brush over the racks of lamb.

• Bake the lamb for 15–20 minutes for rare, or 35 minutes if you prefer medium-rare, brushing with the glaze every 10 minutes. Remove the foil and leave the lamb to stand for 5 minutes before serving with vegetables.

SOUVLAKI

preparation time 20 minutes plus overnight marinating
cooking time 10 minutes
serves 4

1 kg (2 lb 4 oz) boned leg of lamb,
   trimmed and cut into 2 cm
   (¾ inch) cubes
60 ml (2 fl oz/¼ cup) olive oil
2 teaspoons finely grated lemon zest
80 ml (2½ fl oz/⅓ cup) lemon juice
125 ml (4 fl oz/½ cup) dry white wine

2 teaspoons dried oregano
2 large garlic cloves, finely chopped
2 bay leaves
250 g (9 oz/1 cup) Greek-style
   yoghurt
2 garlic cloves, extra, crushed

● If using wooden skewers, soak them in water for 30 minutes to prevent
them from burning during cooking. Put the lamb in a non-metallic bowl with
2 tablespoons of the oil, the lemon zest and juice, wine, oregano, garlic, bay
leaves and some black pepper. Toss, then cover and refrigerate overnight.

● Put the yoghurt and extra garlic in a bowl, mix well and leave for 30 minutes.

● Drain the lamb. Thread onto eight skewers and cook on
a barbecue or chargrill plate, brushing with the remaining
oil, for 7–8 minutes, or until done to your liking.
Serve with the yoghurt, some bread
and a salad.

LAMB FILLETS WITH ZUCCHINI FRITTERS AND TAHINI SAUCE

preparation time 20 minutes plus 1 hour standing
cooking time 15 minutes
serves 2

200 g (7 oz/1½ cups) zucchini
   (courgettes), grated (about 2)
1 egg, lightly beaten
1 brown onion, finely chopped
pinch ground nutmeg
35 g (1¼ oz/¼ cup) plain
   (all-purpose) flour
300 g (10 oz) Greek-style yoghurt
2 teaspoons tahini
1 garlic clove, finely chopped
60 ml (2 fl oz/¼ cup) vegetable oil
½ teaspoon ground cumin

1 teaspoon ground paprika
250 g (9 oz) lamb fillets (about
   3 fillets)
125 g (4 oz) cherry tomatoes, halved
large handful flat-leaf (Italian) parsley
1 teaspoon olive oil

- Preheat the oven to 150°C (300°F/Gas 2).

- Place the zucchini in a colander, sprinkle lightly with salt, then stand for 1 hour to drain. Squeeze as much liquid as possible from the zucchini and place in a bowl. Add the egg, onion, nutmeg, flour and 2 teaspoons water, season to taste with sea salt and freshly ground black pepper and stir to combine well.

- In another bowl, combine the yoghurt, tahini and garlic, season to taste and refrigerate until required.

- Place 2 tablespoons of the vegetable oil in a frying pan over medium–low heat. When the oil is hot, drop spoonfuls of the zucchini mixture into the pan, forming 7.5 cm (3 inch) patties. Cook for 8 minutes, turning once, or until golden and cooked through. Transfer to a baking tray lined with paper towels and place in the oven to keep the patties warm.

- Combine the ground cumin, paprika and ½ teaspoon salt in a small bowl. Wipe the frying pan clean, then place over medium heat. Add the remaining vegetable oil to the pan. Sprinkle the lamb fillets with the spice mix, place in the pan and cook, turning occasionally, for 5 minutes or until golden and just cooked through; the lamb should still be a little pink in the middle.

- Combine the tomatoes, parsley and olive oil in a bowl. Cut the lamb fillets into pieces. Serve with the tomato salad and zucchini fritters. Drizzle the fritters with the tahini sauce and serve immediately.

Meat & fish dishes

SPICED LAMB AND YOGHURT IN PITTA BREAD

preparation time 15 minutes
cooking time 5 minutes
serves 4

2 teaspoons ground cumin
2 teaspoons sweet paprika
2 teaspoons dried oregano
160 ml (5¼ fl oz/⅔ cup) olive oil
160 ml (5¼ fl oz/⅔ cup) lemon juice
800 g (1 lb 12 oz) lamb back strap
500 g (1 lb 2 oz) tin chickpeas,
    rinsed and drained
2 garlic cloves, crushed

160 g (5½ oz/⅔ cup) Greek-style
    yoghurt
4 tablespoons finely chopped mint
2 teaspoons caster (superfine) sugar
4 pitta breads, warmed through
8 baby cos (romaine) lettuce
    leaves, shredded
4 roma (plum) tomatoes, sliced

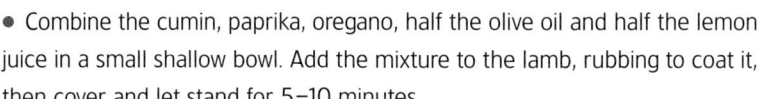

● Combine the cumin, paprika, oregano, half the olive oil and half the lemon
juice in a small shallow bowl. Add the mixture to the lamb, rubbing to coat it,
then cover and let stand for 5–10 minutes.

● Meanwhile, combine the chickpeas with the garlic and the remaining oil and
lemon juice, and 2 tablespoons of warm water in a food processor and process
until a coarse purée forms.

● Place the yoghurt, mint and sugar in a small bowl, mix well to combine, then
set aside.

• Heat a chargrill or frying pan over high heat. Add the lamb and cook for 2−3 minutes each side. Place on a plate and loosely cover with foil for 3 minutes.

• Top the pitta bread with the chickpea purée, shredded lettuce, tomato and sliced lamb. Drizzle with the minted yoghurt and serve immediately, with extra minted yoghurt on the side.

LAMB STEAKS BAKED WITH TOMATO, LENTILS, MINT AND FETA

preparation time 15 minutes
cooking time 25 minutes
serves 4–6

1½ tablespoons olive oil
6 boneless lamb leg steaks (about
    800 g/1 lb 12 oz in total)
1 red onion, sliced into thin rings
2 garlic cloves, crushed
400 g (14 oz) tin chopped tomatoes
400 g (14 oz) tin lentils, rinsed and
    drained

1 small handful small mint leaves
80 g (2¾ oz/½ cup) pitted kalamata
    olives
100 g (3½ oz/⅔ cup) crumbled feta
    cheese

- Preheat the oven to 220°C (425°F/Gas 7).

- Place a large baking dish in the oven to heat for 5 minutes.

- Using a little of the olive oil, brush the lamb on both sides and arrange in a single layer in the hot baking dish. Scatter the onion over the top and bake for 10 minutes.

- Put the remaining oil in a bowl with the garlic, tomatoes, lentils and half the mint. Season to taste with sea salt and freshly ground black pepper and mix well. Spoon the mixture over the lamb and bake for 10 minutes.

- Scatter the olives, feta and remaining mint over the lamb and serve.

LAMB STEAK WITH PECORINO MASH AND ARTICHOKES

preparation time 10 minutes
cooking time 20 minutes
serves 4

8 small desiree potatoes, peeled and
    cut into chunks
160 g (5½ oz) butter
200 ml (7 fl oz) milk
100 g (3½ oz/1 cup) finely grated
    pecorino cheese
60 ml (2 fl oz/¼ cup) olive oil
700 g (1 lb 9 oz) lamb leg steak

500 ml (17 fl oz/2 cups) red wine
8 purchased artichoke hearts in oil,
    drained and quartered
2 garlic cloves, crushed
1 tablespoon lemon juice
4 small handfuls flat-leaf (Italian)
    parsley leaves

Meat & fish dishes

• Cook the potatoes in boiling, salted water for about 10 minutes or until
tender, then drain well. Return to the pan with half of the butter, the milk and
the pecorino. Mash until smooth, then cover with a lid or foil to keep warm.

• Meanwhile, heat 1 tablespoon of the olive oil in a heavy-based frying pan
over high heat. Cook the steaks in batches for 2–3 minutes on each side or
until just cooked through. Remove the steaks from the pan and set aside.

• Add the wine to the pan, stirring to remove any sediment from the base,
then reduce the heat to low and gently boil for 2 minutes. Stir in the remaining
butter and cook for 1–2 minutes, swirling the pan, until glossy. Season to taste
with sea salt and freshly ground black pepper.

• In a small bowl combine the artichoke, garlic, lemon juice, parsley and the
remaining olive oil, and toss to combine. Place the lamb on a serving plate with
the mash and artichokes, and serve immediately with the sauce on the side.

LAMB CHOPS WITH CRUSHED POTATOES, CAPERS AND FETA

preparation time 10 minutes
cooking time 35 minutes
serves 4

8 large lamb loin chops
80 ml (2½ fl oz/⅓ cup) lemon juice
1½ teaspoons dried oregano
2 garlic cloves, crushed
125 ml (4 fl oz/½ cup) olive oil
1 kg (2 lb 4 oz) desiree potatoes,
    peeled and cut into 4 cm (1½ inch)
    chunks

2½ tablespoons capers
150 g (5½ oz/1 cup) crumbled
    feta cheese
1 tablespoon finely grated lemon rind
1 small handful flat-leaf (Italian)
    parsley, chopped
tapenade, to serve

• Preheat the oven to 200°C (400°F/Gas 6).

• Place the lamb chops in a ceramic, glass or stainless steel dish. In a small bowl, mix together the lemon juice, oregano, garlic and 2 tablespoons of the olive oil. Pour over the lamb and set aside for 20 minutes to marinate.

• Meanwhile, place the potatoes in a large saucepan of salted cold water. Bring to the boil and cook for 15 minutes, or until tender. Drain well.

• Place the potatoes in a baking dish and scatter the capers, feta and lemon rind over the top. Drizzle with the remaining olive oil and season with freshly ground black pepper. Roast for 15 minutes, or until golden. Using a potato masher, coarsely crush the potatoes.

• Meanwhile, heat a chargrill pan or barbecue hotplate to medium. Add the lamb chops and cook for 3 minutes on each side, or until done to your liking.

• Divide the potatoes among serving plates and sprinkle the parsley over. Arrange the lamb chops over the top and serve with tapenade.

ROAST LAMB RUMP WITH FENNEL AND CELERIAC REMOULADE

preparation time 20 minutes
cooking time 20 minutes
serves 4

500 g (1 lb 2 oz) trussed cherry
  tomatoes
1 tablespoon vegetable oil
2 x 250 g (9 oz) lamb rumps
  (mini roasts)
60 ml (2 fl oz/¼ cup) lemon juice
1 small celeriac, about 320 g
  (11¼ oz)
1 small fennel bulb, about 225 g
  (8 oz), trimmed and thinly
  sliced widthways

90 g (3¼ oz) whole-egg mayonnaise
1 teaspoon dijon mustard
1 tablespoon drained capers, finely
  chopped
1 tablespoon finely snipped chives

● Preheat the oven to 200°C (400°F/Gas 6).

● Line a baking tray with baking paper. Cut the trussed tomatoes into 4 small
bunches. Place on the baking tray and set aside.

● Heat the oil in a non-stick frying pan over medium heat. Add the lamb rumps
and cook for 2 minutes on each side, or until browned.

● Transfer the lamb to the baking tray with the tomatoes. Roast for 15 minutes,
or until done to your liking. Remove the lamb to a plate, cover loosely with foil
and leave to rest for 5 minutes.

• Meanwhile, add 2 tablespoons of the lemon juice to a bowl of water. Peel and grate the celeriac, adding it to the water as you go to stop it browning. Drain well, then toss the celeriac in a large bowl with the fennel, mayonnaise, remaining lemon juice, mustard, capers and most of the chives.

• Divide the remoulade among serving plates. Carve the lamb rumps and arrange the slices over the remoulade. Sprinkle with the remaining chives and serve with the roasted tomatoes.

LAMB STEAKS WITH WHITE BEAN AND POTATO RAGOUT

preparation time 20 minutes
cooking time 40 minutes
serves 4

2 garlic cloves, peeled
1 rosemary sprig, plus extra leaves,
    to garnish
1 teaspoon finely grated lemon rind
2½ tablespoons lemon juice
60 ml (2 fl oz/¼ cup) olive oil
8 x 100 g (3½ oz) lamb leg steaks
50 g (1¾ oz) pancetta or speck,
    in one piece, finely diced

1 onion, diced
600 g (1 lb 5 oz) Dutch cream or
    nicola potatoes, peeled and cut
    into 1.5 cm (⅝ inch) chunks
250 ml (9 fl oz/1 cup) chicken stock
400 g (14 oz) tinned cannellini beans,
    rinsed and drained
1½ tablespoons chopped flat-leaf
    (Italian) parsley

● In a small bowl, crush the garlic cloves with 1 teaspoon sea salt. Add the rosemary sprig, lemon rind, lemon juice and 1 tablespoon of the olive oil. Mix well, then pour into a large non-metallic dish. Add the lamb and turn to coat all over. Cover and marinate for 30 minutes.

● Heat the remaining oil in a large frying pan over medium–low heat. Add the pancetta and onion and cook for 10–15 minutes, or until the onion is very soft, stirring occasionally.

● Add the potato and cook for a further 3 minutes to absorb the flavours. Pour in the stock and cook for 12–15 minutes, or until the potato is tender. Stir in the cannellini beans and cook for 3 minutes to heat through. Stir in the parsley.

● Meanwhile, preheat a barbecue hotplate or chargrill pan to medium–high. Add the lamb steaks, reduce the heat to medium and cook for 2–3 minutes on each side for medium–rare, or until done to your liking.

● Spoon the bean and potato ragoût onto serving plates or into bowls. Top with the lamb, garnish with extra rosemary and serve.

SAUSAGES WITH POLENTA AND BROCCOLI

preparation time 10 minutes
cooking time 35 minutes
serves 4

1 tablespoon vegetable oil
8 Italian sausages
400 g (14 oz) fennel bulb, thinly
   sliced
1 onion, thinly sliced
250 ml (9 fl oz /1 cup) beef stock

500 ml (17 fl oz/2 cups) chicken stock
500 ml (17 fl oz/2 cups) milk
150 g (5½ oz/1 cup) polenta
250 g (9 oz) broccoli, cut into florets
50 g (1¾ oz/½ cup) grated pecorino
   cheese

● Preheat the oven to 180°C (350°F/Gas 4).

● Heat the oil in a large flameproof casserole dish over medium heat. Add the sausages and cook, turning often, for 5 minutes, or until they are browned all over. Remove to a plate.

● Add the fennel and onion to the dish and sauté for 10 minutes, or until caramelised and golden. Return the sausages to the dish and pour in the beef stock. Transfer to the oven and bake for 15 minutes, or until the sausages are cooked through.

● Meanwhile, combine the chicken stock and milk in a saucepan and heat until simmering. Stirring constantly to prevent any lumps forming, slowly pour in the polenta and bring to a simmer over medium heat. Reduce the heat to low and cook, stirring, for 10–15 minutes, or until the polenta is nearly tender. Remove from the heat, cover and leave to stand for 5 minutes.

● Meanwhile, bring another pan of water to the boil. Add the broccoli and
blanch for 4 minutes, or until just tender. Drain well and keep warm.

● Reheat the sausage and fennel mixture on the stovetop over medium heat
for about 5 minutes, skimming any excess fat from the surface. Serve the hot
polenta with the broccoli, topped with the sausage and fennel mixture.

ROAST PORK WITH HONEY AND POMEGRANATE CARROTS

preparation time 15 minutes
cooking time 25 minutes
serves 4

2 teaspoons ground coriander
2 teaspoons cumin seeds, crushed
large pinch chilli flakes
2 tablespoons olive oil
600 g (1 lb 5 oz) pork tenderloin,
   trimmed
2 bunches baby carrots (about 24),
   trimmed and halved lengthways

1 tablespoon honey
2 teaspoons dijon mustard
80 ml (2½ fl oz/⅓ cup) pomegranate
   molasses
4 handfuls coriander (cilantro) leaves
1 red onion, thinly sliced
80 g (2¾ oz/⅓ cup) Greek-style
   yoghurt

• Preheat the oven to 200°C (400°F/Gas 6). Combine the coriander, cumin seeds, chilli flakes and 1 tablespoon of the olive oil in a large bowl. Coat the pork with the mixture, then set aside.

• Combine the carrots, honey and mustard in a roasting tin and toss to coat the carrot. Season to taste with sea salt and freshly ground black pepper, then roast for 15 minutes, turning the carrot occasionally. Add the molasses to the carrot, tossing to coat, then add the pork, return to the oven and cook for 10 minutes, or until the pork is just cooked through. Remove the pork from the roasting tin, cover loosely with foil and keep warm for 5 minutes.

• Place the coriander leaves, onion and yoghurt in a bowl and gently toss to just combine.

• Place the carrots and sliced pork on warmed serving plates. Add the coriander salad to the plates and serve immediately.

PORK CHOPS IN MARSALA

preparation time 10 minutes
cooking time 15 minutes
serves 4

4 pork loin chops
2 tablespoons olive oil
125 ml (4 fl oz/½ cup) Marsala
2 teaspoons grated orange zest
60 ml (2 fl oz/¼ cup) orange juice
3 tablespoons chopped flat-leaf
   (Italian) parsley

● Pat the pork chops dry and season well. Heat the olive oil in a heavy-based frying pan over medium heat and cook the chops on both sides for 5 minutes each side, or until brown and cooked.

● Add the Marsala, orange zest and juice and cook for 4–5 minutes, or until the sauce has reduced and thickened. Add the parsley and serve.

Meat & fish dishes

HONEY-LIME PORK WITH GINGER SWEET POTATO MASH

preparation time 40 minutes plus 4 hours marinating
cooking time 30 minutes
serves 4

8 thin pork loin steaks or pork
   schnitzels, about **625 g (1 lb 6 oz)**
   in total
25 g (1 oz) butter
80 ml (2½ fl oz/⅓ cup) peanut oil
1 tablespoon finely chopped fresh
   ginger
900 g (2 lb) sweet potatoes, peeled
   and cut into 2 cm (¾ inch) chunks
1½ tablespoons toasted sesame
   seeds (optional)
baby English spinach leaves, to serve

HONEY-LIME MARINADE
1–2 garlic cloves, crushed
1½ tablespoons honey
2 tablespoons Thai sweet chilli sauce
60 ml (2 fl oz/¼ cup) lime juice
1½ tablespoons fish sauce
2 teaspoons sesame oil

● In a small bowl, whisk together the honey-lime marinade ingredients. Pour the mixture into a large bowl, add the pork steaks and toss to coat well. Cover and refrigerate for up to 4 hours.

● Heat the butter and 2 tablespoons of the peanut oil in a saucepan over medium–low heat. Add the ginger and sauté for 2–3 minutes, or until fragrant. Add the sweet potato, stir to coat in the butter mixture, then cover and cook over low heat for 20–25 minutes, or until the sweet potato is very soft, stirring occasionally. Using a potato masher, mash the sweet potato and season to taste with sea salt and freshly ground black pepper. Cover and keep warm.

● Meanwhile, heat the remaining oil in a large frying pan over medium–high heat. Drain the marinated pork, discarding the liquid. Fry the pork in batches for 2 minutes on each side, or until just cooked through.

● Divide the sweet potato mash and pork among serving plates. Sprinkle with the sesame seeds, if using, and serve with baby English spinach leaves.

Meat & fish dishes

JAPANESE PORK STIR-FRY

preparation time 10 minutes
cooking time 20 minutes
serves 4

80 ml (2½ fl oz/⅓ cup) soy sauce
1 tablespoon mirin
1 garlic clove, crushed
1 tablespoon finely grated fresh
    ginger
450 g (1 lb) pork fillet, thinly sliced
2 tablespoons vegetable oil,
    approximately
1 onion, thinly sliced
200 g (7 oz) snow peas (mangetout),
    sliced in half on the diagonal
4 spring onions (scallions), cut into
    long strips
steamed rice, to serve

• In a bowl, combine the soy sauce, mirin, garlic and ginger. Add the pork and toss to coat, then cover and marinate in the refrigerator for 30 minutes. Drain well, reserving the marinade.

• Heat 1 tablespoon of the oil in a wok over high heat. Stir-fry the onion for 5 minutes, or until softened. Remove to a plate using a slotted spoon.

• Heat the remaining oil in the wok. Stir-fry the marinated pork in batches for 2–3 minutes, or until light golden, adding a little more oil as necessary, and removing each batch to a plate.

• Add the reserved marinade to the wok and cook for 2 minutes, or until reduced by half. Return the pork and onion to the wok with the snow peas. Stir-fry for 1–2 minutes, until the snow peas are just tender and the pork is heated through.

• Divide the pork stir-fry among serving bowls. Scatter with the spring onion and serve with steamed rice.

Meat & fish dishes

BAKED SNAPPER WITH LIME-CHILLI DRESSING

preparation time 15 minutes
cooking time 15 minutes
serves 4

6 x 150 g (5½ oz) snapper fillets,
    skin on, pin bones removed
2 cm (¾ inch) piece of fresh ginger,
    peeled and cut into thin
    matchsticks
1 garlic clove, thinly sliced
1 lime, thinly sliced
60 ml (2 fl oz/¼ cup) light soy sauce
2 tablespoons peanut oil
4 baby bok choy (pak choy), halved
    lengthways
3 spring onions (scallions), thinly
    shredded
1 small handful coriander (cilantro)
    leaves
steamed jasmine rice, to serve

LIME-CHILLI DRESSING
60 ml (2 fl oz/¼ cup) lime juice
2 tablespoons soft brown sugar
2 tablespoons fish sauce
1 long red chilli, seeded and finely
    chopped

● Preheat the oven to 200°C (400°F/Gas 6).

● Put the lime-chilli dressing ingredients in a small bowl. Stir until the sugar has
dissolved, then set aside until required.

- Using a small knife, score three lines through the skin of each snapper fillet. Place the fillets in a large baking dish, skin side up, then arrange the ginger, garlic and lime slices over the top. Pour the soy sauce, peanut oil and 250 ml (9 fl oz/1 cup) boiling water over. Bake for 8–10 minutes, or until the fish is just cooked through.

- While the fish is baking, cook the bok choy in a saucepan of salted boiling water for 2 minutes, or until tender.

- Divide the bok choy and fish fillets among serving plates. Garnish with the spring onion and coriander, drizzle with the lime–chilli dressing and serve with the steamed jasmine rice.

SMOKED FISH WITH HORSERADISH CREAM SAUCE

preparation time 10 minutes
cooking time 25 minutes
serves 4–6

1.25 kg (2 lb 12 oz) smoked fish
   fillets, such as cod
1 tablespoon vegetable oil
50 g (1¾ oz) butter
1 onion, finely diced
1 leek, white part only, rinsed well
   and finely diced
50 g (1¾ oz/½ cup) plain
   (all-purpose) flour
2 tablespoons bottled horseradish,
   or to taste

100 ml (3½ fl oz) cream
steamed spinach, to serve
boiled potatoes, to serve
2 tablespoons snipped chives

POACHING STOCK
600 ml (21 fl oz) milk
1 onion, sliced
1 carrot, sliced
1 bay leaf

● Put the poaching stock ingredients in a large shallow saucepan or deep frying pan with 400 ml (14 fl oz) water. Bring to the boil. Add the fish, then reduce the heat to low and simmer for 10 minutes, until the fish is tender.

● Reserving the poaching stock, remove the fish to a warm bowl. Cover with a sheet of greased baking paper and keep warm.

● Heat the oil and butter in a saucepan over medium heat. Add the onion and leek and sauté for 5 minutes, or until softened. Sprinkle the flour over the onion mixture and cook, stirring, for 1 minute, or until smooth.

● Strain 500 ml (17 fl oz/2 cups) of the poaching stock into the saucepan. Stir over medium–low heat for 5 minutes, or until thickened. Stir in the horseradish and cream and season to taste with sea salt and freshly ground black pepper.

● Serve the fish with steamed spinach and boiled potatoes, drizzled with the horseradish cream sauce and sprinkled with the chives.

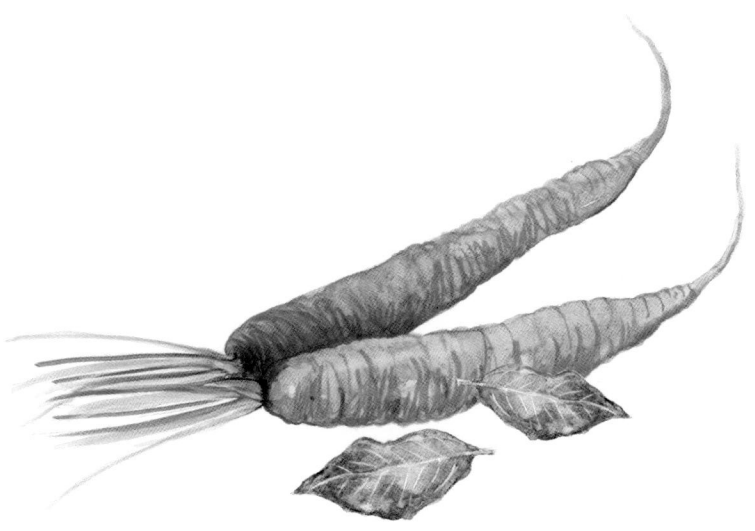

RUSTIC FISH STEW

preparation time 30 minutes plus soaking time
cooking time 15 minutes
serves 6

1 kg (2 lb 4 oz) small clams (vongole)
30 g (1 oz) butter
1 large onion, finely chopped
2 celery stalks, chopped
2 carrots, finely chopped
2 thyme sprigs
125 ml (4 fl oz/½ cup) white wine
375 ml (13 fl oz/1½ cups) chicken
   stock
1 kg (2 lb 4 oz) ling fillets, or other
   firm white fish fillets, thickly sliced

800 g (1 lb 12 oz) raw king prawns
   (shrimp), peeled and deveined,
   tails left intact
2 vine-ripened tomatoes, finely
   chopped
1 small handful dill, finely chopped
aïoli, to serve
crusty bread, to serve
lemon wedges, to serve

• Place the clams in a bowl and cover with plenty of cold water. Cover and refrigerate for 2–3 hours. Drain the clams, discarding any that are open.

• Melt the butter in a large heavy-based saucepan over medium–high heat. Add the onion, celery, carrot and thyme sprigs and sauté for 5 minutes, or until the vegetables have softened.

• Pour in the wine and bring to the boil. Reduce the heat to low, then simmer for 5 minutes, or until half the wine has evaporated.

• Pour in the stock and 250 ml (9 fl oz/1 cup) water. Return to the boil, then reduce the heat to low. Add the fish, prawns and clams. Cover and simmer for 3–4 minutes, shaking the pan occasionally.

● Remove the pan from the heat. Leave the lid on and allow to stand for 3 minutes, or until the clams have opened and all the seafood is cooked through. Remove and discard any clams that haven't opened.

● Stir the tomato and dill into the remaining stew, then divide among serving bowls. Top each bowl with aïoli, then serve with crusty bread and lemon wedges.

Meat & fish dishes

FISH BAKED IN PAPER

preparation time 10 minutes

cooking time 25 minutes

serves 6

600 g (1 lb 5 oz) fresh rice noodles

3 large bok choy (pak choy), leaves
trimmed, separated and cut in half

200 g (7 oz) snow peas (mangetout),
trimmed and thinly sliced
lengthways

6 x 150 g (5½ oz) firm white fish
fillets, such as ling or monk fish

4 spring onions (scallions), trimmed
and thinly sliced on the diagonal

2 tablespoons very thinly sliced fresh
ginger

125 ml (4 fl oz/½ cup) soy sauce

125 ml (4 fl oz/½ cup) Chinese rice
wine

● Preheat the oven to 180°C (350°F/Gas 4).

● Cut six sheets of baking paper about 30 cm (12 inches) square. Lay the
sheets on a work surface and divide the noodles among them, placing the
noodles in the middle of each sheet and spreading them slightly to form a
single layer.

● Divide the bok choy and snow peas among the noodles, then place a fish
fillet on each. Sprinkle with the spring onion, ginger, soy sauce and rice wine.
Fold the short ends of the paper in over the fish, then double-fold the long
edges together to seal and form tight parcels.

● Place the parcels on a baking tray and bake for 20–25 minutes, or until
the fish is cooked through and the vegetables are tender. Divide the parcels
among warm plates and serve.

WHOLE FISH STEAMED WITH CHINESE FLAVOURS

preparation time 10 minutes

cooking time 10 minutes

serves 4

1.6 kg (3 lb 8 oz) whole baby
    barramundi or snapper, cleaned
    and scaled
4 spring onions (scallions), finely sliced
3 garlic cloves, sliced
1 tablespoon finely sliced fresh ginger
80 ml (2½ fl oz/⅓ cup) light soy sauce
2 tablespoons sesame oil
1 tablespoon caster (superfine) sugar
2 teaspoons cornflour (cornstarch)
steamed rice, to serve

GARNISH
4 spring onions (scallions), finely sliced
coriander (cilantro) leaves
2 large red chillies, seeded and
    thinly sliced, or to taste

• Place a large bamboo steamer in a large frying pan or wok, add water to the pan so it comes just to the base of the steamer; the water should not touch the steamer. Bring the water to the boil. Line the steamer with baking paper and place the fish on top of the paper.

• Combine the spring onion, garlic, ginger, soy sauce, sesame oil, sugar and cornflour in a small bowl and stir to mix well. Spoon the mixture over the fish, cover and steam for 8–10 minutes or until the fish is just cooked through.

• Garnish with the spring onion, coriander and chilli slices and serve with steamed rice on the side.

Meat & fish dishes

Index